D1452879

Partial Recall

BOOKS BY JOHN D. VERDERY

Partial Recall:

The Afterthoughts of a Schoolmaster   *1981*

It's Better to Believe   *1964*

John D. Verdery

PARTIAL RECALL

The Afterthoughts of a Schoolmaster

ATHENEUM

New York

1981

92
V583

81 12083

Library of Congress Cataloging in Publication Data

Verdery, John D.
    Partial recall.

    1. Verdery, John D. 2. School superintendents and
principals—Connecticut—Danbury—Biography. 3. Protestant Episcopal Church in the U.S.A.—Clergy—Biography.
4. Clergy—United States—Biography. 5. Wooster School
—History—Addresses, essays, lectures. I. Title.
LD7501.D168V475   1981   373.12′012′0924 [B]   81-66007
ISBN 0-689-11207-6   AACR2

T O

JOSEPH GROVER, DONALD SCHWARTZ, *and* HOBART WARNER, *who have, among them, shared 120 years of their lives with me as friends and fellow workers*

Contents

Partial Recall

Preface

———————◆———————

WHEN I was elected headmaster of Wooster School, in Danbury, Connecticut, two months before my twenty-sixth birthday, I made the mistake of boasting about it to my father. "You know, Dad," I said, "I am not sure, but I think I'm the youngest headmaster in America." My father, who had three sons, none of whom he took too seriously, replied, "Well, son, you'd better get some other virtue, because that one won't last long."

By playing my cards carefully, and trying to follow my father's advice, I eventually reached the point where I might have boasted to my father again, if he had still been alive, "You know, Dad, I'm not sure, but I think I am one of the *oldest* headmasters in America." To which I am sure my father would have said the same thing.

The years in between have supplied me with the raw material for this book; but it is not a book about a New England independent school headmaster. That is merely (to use one of those overworked phrases of the moment) "where I'm coming from." As a schoolmaster and a priest, as well as a minor-league administrator of a nonprofit corporation, I have coped with the problems that most people face, have dealt with them, and have reached some conclusions. If I had ended up, as I had once planned, as rector of a parish, I probably would have found more or less the same problems and probably reached more or less the same conclusions. And if I had followed my grandmother's advice, after she had read my horoscope, and become an engineer, the same would no doubt have held true. The one special thing about my condition is that the overwhelming majority of the people I have lived and worked with have been young and, unlike me, have continued to be young.

As far as wisdom is concerned, my major claim to it rests on the simple fact that I have lived longer than some people, and even that is watered down by the nature of my two specialties, religion and education— two areas in which almost everyone considers himself wise. I do have a reputation for being more or less well adjusted; but this proposition was once put into perspective by my aunt. Jokingly, I asked her one day if perhaps the reason I am so well adjusted is that I am really not very smart. She thought about it for a moment and then said, with no smile but with an ever-so-slight twinkle in her eye, "Yes." Every aunt is entitled to her own opinion, and I think her secret agenda was my ego.

In December of 1942, the Reverend Aaron Coburn, founder and first headmaster of Wooster School, died of a heart attack. A few evenings later, I got a phone call from his son, John, my close friend and seminary classmate. He said, "How would you like to be headmaster of Wooster School?" Having just graduated from seminary the spring before, having spent the summer running a boys' camp not altogether happily, having just started my first job in the parish ministry the previous September, having a wife who was finishing her last year of college, my first reaction was totally negative. I didn't even believe that John was serious. In addition, I had some deep-seated feelings about the war that was in progress, about my responsibilities to my conscience and to my country, feelings that had been hammered out to a very great extent in seminary with friends like John. I had plans to respond to those feelings by enlisting in the navy as a chaplain. And finally, I was scared. What possible basis could there be for anyone to think that I could be headmaster of a New England independent school at that point in my life?

John spent the following six weeks trying to sell me to the board of trustees and trying to sell the idea to me.

My wife, Suzanne, and I were living in a small apartment in Boston, from which I walked to work at St. Paul's Episcopal Cathedral and she commuted to Wellesley College. I was interviewed for the Wooster job by the president of the board in the Massachusetts General Hospital. It was the morning after the terrible Cocoanut Grove fire, and Dr. Allen O. Whipple, the board president, had flown up from New York the night before as an expert on the treatment of burns. He was a man of such great spiritual depth, and the setting was so dramatic, that he managed to put a good many of my fears and misgivings to rest. Nevertheless, Sue and I arrived on the Wooster campus on January 9, 1943, with our minds still not wholly made up. At one point John came out of the meeting, called me aside, and said, "You know, John, it would be a lot easier for me to get you this job if you would tell me if you want it or not." As a final stall, I once again expressed my fear that I did not think that I was up to having his father's life work entrusted to me. John said, "Why don't you try it for five years, and if the school closes, what the hell, it probably would have closed anyway."

That night at dinner I was introduced to the students as the new headmaster. I made a little speech, and I still have no idea what I said. All I could see was an enormous army of blurred boys' faces, jammed shoulder to shoulder in a huge hall. Later I learned that there were only fifty boys and the room was exactly forty-eight feet long. One member of the senior class was nineteen years old and my wife was twenty-one, and I found out later that to the boys, my wife was the most impressive thing about me.

Of course it was not all quite so simple and haphazard. The soil upon which this most unexpected seed fell had not been entirely unprepared. I had always been a hero worshipper, and at Blair Academy, in the tenth grade, I had had an English teacher who became one of my heroes. His name was Theodore Roosevelt Jeffers, indicating that his father must have been something of a hero worshipper too. I liked everything about this man and thought to my fifteen-year-old self, "I'd like to be like him. I'd like to be a teacher." Then I met another hero, the Reverend Donald B. Aldrich, rector of the Church of the Ascension in New York City. I liked everything about him too, and so said to my still-fifteen-year-old self, "I'd like to be like him. I'd like to be a clergyman." All through the rest of my school days and through college, I kept both options open in my mind. It didn't seem to me that they were so very different, or that there was any great rush about making up my mind. When it came time to go to theological seminary, I just went, thinking by this time that if I were to be a teacher, I'd rather teach religion than anything else. What never occurred to me for one minute was to be the clerical headmaster of a church school. And when the idea was presented, it took me time to realize that this was a perfect marriage of the two interests of my young life. The signs of life are most easily read in the rearview mirror.

Running the boys' camp right after having graduated from seminary (and five days after getting married) contributed something to my blindness. It was an awful summer. The camp was owned by St. Paul's Cathedral and run for its boys' choir. The campers were not so bad and were kept busy part of every day by the cathedral organist, a delightful German refugee by the name of Ludwig Theis. He and Thomas Messer, a Czechoslovak refugee about my age (who would one day be the director of the Guggenheim Museum and would continue to be my friend for life and eventually serve as a trustee of Wooster), helped keep Sue and me sane. But because of the war, almost every male American over eighteen was in the service, and with one or two exceptions, in addition to my two refugee friends, the counselors were the most inept, immature, irresponsible, inexperienced, and unqualified teen-age boys who had ever been assembled to do anything. The result was that at the end of the summer, I said to Sue as we were driving back to Boston, "One thing is sure. I don't ever again want anything to do with teen-age boys. That's settled." Of course, it wasn't, but it took me a little time to make the emotional adjustment to the idea of spending the rest of my life with them.

My father, who was an alumnus of Lawrenceville, was more alarmed than pleased or proud when he got the news of my appointment. He immediately called his old school's headmaster, Allan Heely. "Allan," he said, "I need your help. My son has just done a terrible thing. He has accepted a job as headmaster of a school, and, Allan, *he doesn't know anything!*" Allan Heely, with a school of more than five hundred boys, promised to take a couple of days off to visit Wooster and give my father a report. This he did, thereby becoming another of my heroes and my favorite among the then older generation of headmasters. Later on there were others who were similarly helpful in my early days of innocence: George Van Santvoord of Hotchkiss, Paul Cruickshank of Taft, Nelson Hume of Canterbury, and Sam Bartlett of South Kent. Their motto seemed to be "Let's help Verdery. *He doesn't know anything.*"

What my father and those other headmasters were assuming was all too obvious to everyone on the Wooster campus. I really didn't know anything. I had never taught a class in my life, and my only administrative job had been a horrendous disaster. It would be five years before I would have a single employee younger than myself. My only asset was that I, too, along with everyone else, knew that I didn't know anything. Sam Bartlett gave me my cue: "John, whenever you find anyone in your school who can do something better than you can, get down on your knees and thank God, and let him do it."

This I did. There had been two months between Dr. Coburn's death and my starting as headmaster, on February 14, during which time the school had somehow run fairly well without any headmaster. Sue was back on the Wellesley campus finishing her last term, and I was living temporarily in a two-room dormitory apartment. For that whole first spring I just stood around and watched people do things and tried to figure out what it was that *I* was supposed to be doing.

Thirty-four years later, when I resigned as headmaster, I knew the answer; a headmaster's job, or the job of any top administrator, is to see that he is always surrounded by people who can do the things that need to be done better than he and to try to keep them happy doing those things. He must also learn how to interpret the institution, its mission and purpose, to all employees and customers and to the outside world. Beyond that, his main job is to stay out of the way and, like a major-league baseball manager, always take the rap for anything that goes wrong and give the credit to others when things go right.

During those first months, in spite of my desire to remain on the sidelines, there were a couple of issues that I had to deal with almost right away. One was presented to me by the faculty on my first day in office. It seemed that a boy named Carpenter, who had already been guilty of several rule infractions, had stolen some coffee from the kitchen a few weeks before, and the faculty had been waiting impatiently for a new headmaster to decide what to do about it. The real issue was the reestablishment of discipline in general, since it seemed to have slipped somewhat during the school's headmasterless period. I announced that since I had never seen the boy and knew nothing about the circumstances, I would leave the whole matter up to a faculty vote. Whatever they decided to do, I would carry out. To my horror, they decided that the boy should be expelled. So I expelled him. His parents, needless to say, were not too pleased with the new headmaster, and neither was I. I resolved never again to leave that kind of decision to a faculty vote. Nevertheless, the important point had been made that the faculty in any such institution *should* have *something* to say about the running of it. This was a new idea at

Wooster, and it caused one veteran teacher (a veteran of many institutions) to say to me, with his arms folded across his chest, staring out my living-room window, "You know, Verdery, you're the best headmaster I ever worked for. But I suppose in a couple of years you'll be a son of a bitch just like all the rest of them." At that moment I felt pretty pleased with myself. Later on, when I realized all that he meant, I was only half pleased with myself.

The next issue with which I was confronted was more difficult. I was told that a female member of the staff, age twenty-one and married to a GI who was overseas, had seduced five members of the senior class. What to do? Even I could figure out that she had to go. But what about the boys? On the one hand, the school was obviously at fault for allowing the conditions that made the seductions possible, and who could blame a normal teen-age boy, closeted in a boys' school, for succumbing to such a temptation? When the young Thomas Aquinas was confronted with a similar situation, he jumped out of bed, grabbed a burning log out of the fireplace with the fire tongs, drove the young lady in question screaming from his room, slammed the door behind her, and then made a huge sign of the cross on it with the burning log, threw the log back into the fireplace, and got back into bed. But he was a saint, and most schoolboys are not.

On the other hand, it was argued, those boys were an undeniable embarrassment to the community. The same teacher who had earlier praised me stood up suddenly during the faculty meeting and, pulling huge clumps of hair out of his head with his two hands, shouted, "What the hell do you have to *do* to get kicked out of this goddamned school?" So we found a way to compromise. They all left school, but returned after graduation, took their exams, and were all awarded diplomas. My father christened the young lady "the student body," and John Coburn commiserated with me.

The next problem arrived shortly thereafter. The very first teacher I hired that spring was a homosexual. I was scared. I really didn't have the goods on him. All I knew for sure was that the boys had decided he was. Suppose I were to accuse him and fire him and he were to sue me. I called him into my office and told him that I didn't know whether he was a homosexual or not, but that the boys thought so, and therefore I didn't see how he could go on teaching. Then I held my breath. He was, of course, much older than I and a very bright European.

He said, "Yes, of course I'm a homosexual. But I don't see what that has to do with my teaching. Socrates was a homosexual."

Once again we reached a compromise. He left. Much later, but long before homosexuals began to assert their rights in society, I developed my own theory about homosexual teachers in boys' schools. They are no worse than, and no different from, heterosexual teachers in coed schools. The question is not what one's preference may be, but whether or not one behaves. Both heterosexual and homosexual teachers come in two forms: moral and immoral. A school is a bad place for an immoral teacher.

From the very first day there was one duty that I assigned to myself—to conduct services of worship in the school chapel. After all, I had spent three years in a theological seminary and I was *supposed* to know how to do that. And I liked it. Beginning right away, and for the next twenty-five years, until we hired our first school chaplain, I conducted all services of worship whenever I was on campus, seven days a week. It was not merely a routine. It was my teaching post. (I never taught in the classroom.) It was a position from which I carried out what I saw to be my first responsibility, to interpret the institution and its mission, over and over again.

Not unnaturally, since I had established a corner on the chancel and pulpit, I found myself little by little becoming a pastor to an ever-increasing congregation of young people, and their parents, and some members of the faculty, and their children. I baptized people and married people, and, alas, even in a school for the young, I buried people. Parents send their children to church schools for a variety of reasons, some of which have nothing to do with religion. The variety of reasons led, increasingly, year after year, to a great variety of students. More often than not they did *not* come from churchgoing families. I became their pastor because I was the only clergyman they knew. I discovered, to my surprise, that I was a missionary.

This does not mean that I ever became very interested in *converting* anyone to the Christian faith, let alone the Episcopal Church. A Jewish girl came to me one day and accused me of "brainwashing" her.

"Sarah," I said, "I'm not brainwashing you. I am trying to provide you with the one thing in the world that can keep you from ever being brainwashed. I am trying to force you to confront the fact that sooner or later you have to decide what you believe . . . that it matters."

A few weeks later she came to me again and said, "The brainwashing has worked! I want to be baptized a Christian."

"What does your rabbi say?" I asked.

"I haven't seen him in several years. I left confirmation class without finishing."

"Let's go see him together and talk the whole thing over."

"No," she said, "I'd rather go alone."

She did, and went back to her Jewish confirmation class and finished.

Many years earlier, during one of my first years as a headmaster, a boy came to me with the same question. He was also Jewish, but not a practicing Jew. I told him that I would be glad to baptize him, but only if he would wait a year, until after his graduation. I said that I was pleased that he liked the Wooster chapel, but what he proposed to join was much bigger than that. I also suggested that when he came back he bring his father with him. During his freshman year in college, to my surprise, he met both conditions. His father was frank.

"Well, Jason," he said, "if you want to be baptized a Christian, it's O.K. with me; but if you think anyone's going to stop thinking you're Jewish, you're crazy."

The son agreed with his father, but wanted, nevertheless, to be baptized. So I baptized him, and later married him and baptized all his children. These two experiences helped me to realize that my job was to confront young people with my faith in such a way as to make them think about the importance of developing one of their own.

In 1943 Wooster was an Episcopal Church school, not by corporate ties, but by self-definition and commitment. There were fifty students, all boys, all boarding, all white, and most of them Episcopalians. Because of the school's liberal scholarship policy, they were not all from the same social or economic set, not like the Groton that Francis Biddle describes in *A Casual Past*, where, he reports, 90 percent of the students' families were in the *Social Register*. But both institutions inherited their traditions from the English public schools. At Wooster the boys wore coats and ties to all meals and all classes, and wore a dark blue suit and a white shirt to chapel on Sundays. They never went home for weekends and rarely got into town. Every boy in the school played football. Their ambition, if they could survive the war that hung over them (and some did not), was to go to an Ivy League college. A great many did.

In 1976, when I resigned as headmaster, Wooster was still an Episcopal Church school, by the same definition, but with very different outward and visible signs and practices. It had an enrollment of 270 students, boys and girls in almost equal numbers, some of whom were blacks, Chicanos, Orientals, Jews, and Puerto Ricans. Some of them were day students, and all of them enjoyed a certain freedom on weekends. They dressed much like their high school contemporaries. Only a small minority played football, and an even smaller minority were Episcopalians. An even smaller minority went on to Ivy League colleges.

During the thirty-four years that the school was changing, the world was also changing. There were three wars—each with its own effect on society as a whole, as well as on a New England boarding school campus. Television, jumbo jets, computers, rock music, and nuclear energy appeared in everyone's life. Some time-honored values turned out to be timeworn. University and even independent school campuses were shaken to their foundations by a new kind of revolution in the 1960s. Martin Luther King, Jr., the Berrigan brothers, the Kennedy brothers, Angela Davis, William Sloane Coffin, Jr., Dr. Spock, Richard Nixon, and many others—some heroes, some villains, and everything in between—changed the lives of almost every American in one way or another.

And I changed too. Scared as I was at the prospect before me in 1943, I actually had more self-confidence then (which is to say less modesty) than I had in 1976. In some ways I did fulfill my colleague's prediction. I did become a son of a bitch, at least in the eyes of some. Life turned out to be more complicated than I had thought, anchors to windward less secure. The faith that had been born in my youth, and nurtured in seminary, and brought so carefully to the school where I was to spend my entire professional life—so neat and tidy—has never deserted me. But I have often found myself wrapping it around things and circumstances instead of wrapping things and circumstances around my faith, the way I had been led to believe I could. I had thought my faith would shape my life; but I have learned that sometimes my life has shaped my faith.

What happens to the dreams of one's youth? Most young people have more or less good dreams. They are idealistic, optimistic, heroic, and they want to save the world. When they get out into the world they find that it is not so easy, and they make adjustments—some good and some bad, some they are ashamed of and some they are proud of, some conscious and some unconscious. And sometimes they discover that their early dreams were not good enough, and they have better ones later on. I have a good memory for the dreams of my youth. They meant a great deal to me while I was dreaming them, and they still do. I also know what happened to those dreams between the ages of fifteen and sixty-five. In a sense my life could be anybody's.

Even the specifics have a kind of general relevance. Not everyone has been involved in the life of a New England independent school, as I have been; but everyone has had to grow up and be taught, and a great many people have had some sort of involvement in the growing up of others—as parents, or teachers, or trustees, or school board members, or neighbors of people with children.

I have tried not to preach (at least I keep telling myself that I have tried), but I am a preacher and of course the title of the book, *Partial Recall,* is obviously meant to imply two things: that I do not have total recall and that I have unabashedly remembered what I wanted to.

A Decent Docent Dassn't Doze

A decent docent dassn't doze,
Must do his teaching
On his toes.
A student dassn't doze,
But does.
And that's what education is . . .
And was.

Spike Adriance, for many years a member of the
Andover faculty, taught me that little poem one day
when I met him at the Desert Museum, outside Tucson,
Arizona, where he was enjoying his first years of retirement—as a docent. A docent usually means a museum
guide, but the word can also be used as a generic term
for teacher. It seems to me that this poem summarizes
rather neatly what education is all about and what it
has always been about. As I soon learned after coming
to Wooster, the trick is to find teachers who are awake
and who know how to keep students awake.

17

Among teen-age Americans, there are a lot of ways of dozing, a lot of reasons for not paying attention. In an article in the *New York Times* on June 13, 1979, entitled "The Classroom's Ubiquitous Rival: Pop Culture," Clifton Fadiman wrote: "Of course, [our children] still obey the authority of the educational system. But they have no inner commitment to it. Good teachers . . . almost always finally admit that their difficulties stem from the competition of the alternate life (T.V., etc.). And this competition they are not trained to meet. The alternate life has one special psychological effect that handicaps the teacher—any teacher. . . . That effect is a decline in the faculty of attention, and therefore, a decline in the capacity to learn."

I agree with Mr. Fadiman that in degree and special cause, this is a problem peculiar to our time. But in lesser degree and for a variety of other reasons, attracting and holding the attention of young people has always been a problem. They do have a tendency to doze. In fact, wanting to pay attention and wanting to follow instructions are two such rare characteristics of adolescence that Bernard Shaw was just about right when he said, "Youth is a wonderful thing. What a crime to waste it on children." Certainly it is no time to get educated.

The principle of education is so simple. I may have learned something valuable the hard way, through experience, through trial and error, and in order to save you from having to go through the same laborious and perhaps painful process, I'll just tell you about it! The idea is efficiency, so that each generation will not have to learn everything from the bottom up. I have a friend who worked out the Pythagorean theorem on his own when he was twelve years old. He had heard that Einstein had done it, so he felt he had to. But for most people that isn't a very practical way to learn it. Pythagoras worked it out for all future generations. Unless you happen to be a genius, why not take advantage of that fact?

This oversimplified theory of education doesn't work because people would rather learn for themselves. One has only to picture the five-year-old boy getting for Christmas a new toy that has to be put together according to directions. His father immediately takes it from him and starts to show him how it is done, whereupon the child starts to cry and stamp his foot and grab at the toy until he finally breaks it. When that child becomes an adolescent, he has not changed a whole lot. Either he still wants to figure the thing out for himself, or he is not interested in the project at all. He has something else on his mind, which could be *almost anything*. When he is ready, he will learn fast and easily; but until he is ready, he is virtually unteachable. That is why my own concern with education has been almost entirely with the student and his problems, rather than with the academic curriculum. The new math didn't interest me any more than the old math. Whether or not our school dropped Latin never seemed to me to matter a great deal. I always left curriculum revolutions to someone else. I do not mean to imply that these questions are unimportant, or that at Wooster we were not concerned about them. We have a curriculum committee that meets regularly all year long, every year, constantly revising and honing what shall be taught. But from my standpoint, what kept me in the school world for a lifetime was the care and feeding of the teen-age psyche.

I could never see how this could be done except in some religious context or other. The concern is for the well-being of a human soul, at a time when it is particularly vulnerable. To me that is a religious concern. Once, some years back, when private educational institutions of all sorts were being threatened with extinction (not collectively, but individually), a friend of mine from Yale said to me over a Christmas cup, "What's Wooster doing to survive?" I said, without thinking, "We're a church school. What's Yale doing to survive?" He hitched his belt up with his two thumbs and said, "You may be right." The separation of religion and education, however necessary for political reasons in America, is a sad loss—at least for adolescents. It *is* possible that in the long run religion will be the one reason for private educational institutions to survive. The so-called public sector can do everything else as well as the private sector, if it wants to. That it often doesn't want to, or finds it politically too difficult, is another matter.

Church schools, or religious schools, come in all forms and styles. Some are corporately connected with a parish or a diocese, or a province. Some are under the authority of a national church. Some, like Wooster, have no corporate ties, only a self-definition in their charters. In the final analysis a church school is one that says it is, like a baptized person of any Christian community. In the old Episcopal baptismal service were the words that the child to be baptized "not be ashamed to confess the faith of Christ crucified." That's all there is to it. But that is nonetheless a distinguishing characteristic. There are many independent schools that have many of the same religious trappings as church schools; the difference is that they do not choose to confess any particular faith. A non-church school may have, but a church school must have some kind of regular corporate worship with some sort of recognizable form. Religion, like anything else, involves some knowledge, and corporate worship involves a certain amount of *common* knowledge. That means routine, and in the case of the music, even practice. Such things tend to be no more popular among the young than any other kind of homework.

At Wooster we have experienced no less bitching about "compulsory chapel" than any other such school. And through the years we have had our demonstrations of boredom and even hostility. One boy, many years ago, not out of zeal but for reasons of sabotage, simply shouted "Amen" at the top of his lungs at the end of a prayer. The whole congregation sat bolt upright and the mood of the moment was destroyed. The form of his sabotage was so original, and so delightfully hard to deal with, that I almost burst out laughing. He had me cold! What's wrong with saying "Amen" with spirit? In some churches people do it all the time. I didn't know for sure who it was, but ten years later he wrote me a letter confessing and apologizing. The reason for the sabotage was anger or boredom over having to be there; and the reason for apology ten years later was that being there had not been totally meaningless.

Written on the inside of the door of our chapel, in gold letters in English, Spanish, and French, are the words "Believers, say a prayer. Unbelievers, be respectful." Since the pews face each other and not the front, the words are easy for anyone to read at any time during a service. They had not yet been written on the door when my young friend was a student, but ten years later he had figured out the idea for himself.

All religions need "outward and visible signs," whether in the form of a worship service, or a building, or grace at meals, or vestments, or certain kinds of holidays other than Christmas and Easter—such as All Saints Day, Ash Wednesday, Good Friday, or Pentecost. I think such things are meaningful to young people. We once had a monk come and preach for us, and the boys almost revolted at the very idea. He opened his sermon by saying, "I am a monk. That is someone who dresses like mother, is called father, and hasn't any children at all." Everyone laughed, and he did very well. But what impressed the boys most was that after the service was over, he simply got down on his knees, as everyone was leaving, and said his own prayers. The boy whose job it was to clean the chapel hesitated in the wings, whereupon the monk, from his knees, in the midst of his prayers, said, "Go ahead and do your cleaning. You won't bother either me or God."

But, of course, with the "outward and visible signs" there must also be the "inward and spiritual grace." Church schools have gotten a bad name because they have not been sufficiently different from non-church schools. They have not been leaders in the realm of racial integration, or in achieving social and economic mixes among their students. They have displayed no more patience and forgiveness in dealing with matters of discipline than their secular counterparts. They have too often worshipped at the shrine of intellectual excellence and admission to prestigious colleges. What church schools do have in their favor, which some of them have used to their credit, is the means of self-criticism. There is that Bible! And if you take it seriously, you have to take it very seriously.

I went to one of the original progressive schools in America, in New York City, from 1921 to 1931. In all of its educational methods it was years ahead of its time. By comparison, the Wooster I came to in 1943 was antediluvian. My grammar school principal was horrified, not only because I had entered the church, but because, as a priest, I had entered the field of education, where, in her opinion, I could only do harm. She once told a friend that I was one of two failures in the history of her school, the other having landed in reform school. But when I went back to that school forty-one years later, I found to *my* horror that it had not changed one bit, that the school where I worked was infinitely more progressive. What did it was theology. It was our theology, our basis for self-criticism, that saved us from ourselves. It was that Bible! You can't keep reading it, especially in public, before young people, and ever feel self-satisfied.

But the saving of an institution is not the main point. "Inward and spiritual grace" is primarily needed for the young people in our care. The ultimate goal is a sane adult with a touch of zeal for improving the world. The instruments are a sense of community and all the time that it takes, not just in terms of hours and days and weeks, but in terms of years. For me this means a boarding school. Since the American boarding school is a relatively rare bird, however, it can't be the answer for everyone.

Educational philosophers talk these days about educating the "whole child." I find that an unattractive phrase, but I guess it says more or less what I mean. The twenty-four-hour day is hard to beat with that as the goal. The community is a fact, whether supportive or not. And the time is there, though often the claims on it are hard to meet. In such a community, with an around-the-clock schedule, there are bound to be times and circumstances when the student doesn't doze—and so can be taught.

Consider death. A lot of independent schools these days are teaching courses in death and dying. I helped teach one myself, as a kind of guest expert, and think the idea a good one. But finally, death teaches itself as nothing else can; and it enters the lives of the young far more frequently than might be supposed; and because it often comes as a stranger, it hits very hard.

The time is eleven o'clock at night, and the phone rings. It is a Mr. Jones, whom I don't know, calling on behalf of Mrs. Monroe. It seems that Mr. Monroe dropped dead in the railroad station on his way home from work. Would I be so kind as to break the news to his son, David? I decide to wait till the next morning, go to breakfast at school, wait till David has finished his breakfast, find David's girl friend and tell her what I am about to do, and then call David in. "David, I have bad news for you." I allow only a slight pause, while he looks up at me in some fright. "Your father is dead. He died of a heart attack on his way home from work last night."

This is an assignment that I have been asked to do many times. The approach has been carefully thought out, and the key is abruptness—like death itself. But it is not something that anyone gets good at, just because he has been asked to do it before. There is no way to predict what the reaction will be, whether the session will last half an hour or half the morning. What is sure is that the student isn't dozing and that sometimes, therefore, some helpful things can be said—about fatherhood and sonship, about mothers, about the meaning of life, about the loneliness of sorrow, maybe . . . just maybe . . . something about faith.

Invariably the community rallies 'round. The young man discovers that he has friends he didn't know about. His friends discover that they care in a way they didn't realize. There is a brief chapel service, after David has gone home to be with his family, and everyone finds out that some of those boring words they had been

repeating, so often that they know them by heart, have
special meaning.

The first time death struck the Wooster campus was
when Aaron Coburn, the founder and first headmaster,
himself died. He had gone to New York for the day to
see his doctor, had a heart attack, and died. I was, of
course, not associated with the school at the time, but
the scene has often been described to me. The word hit
the campus, and of course everyone was stunned. What
to do? It was not a faculty member but the head of the
student body who made the first move. He rang the
chapel bell, and at age seventeen, with very little previous experience, conducted a service of worship for the
community. He then continued to conduct all chapel
services every day until I became headmaster, two
months later.

Another example: The whole school is in the dining
room having lunch, and through the window they can
see one of the school pickup trucks come slowly around
the corner of the kitchen, headed for the chapel. It is
being driven by Tony Romeo, a member of the school
maintenance staff. To everyone's horror, as the truck
heads toward the chapel, it does not stop, until it has
crashed into the side of the building. Tony is slumped
over the steering wheel, dead from a heart attack. A
young faculty member tries to revive him, to no avail.
Two hundred and seventy young people, for a few days
at least, have an opportunity to get their own problems into some sort of perspective. And even after those
few days, they will never be quite the same again.

A third example: A boy in the junior class goes to
the infirmary with a sore throat, during exam week,
just before Christmas. A day later he is moved to the
hospital. Then word comes back that his condition is

critical, and, during the Christmas party, the school learns of his death. Most students have already left for home before the news can reach them. But others volunteer to try to telephone everyone. The funeral, a few days later, is held in the boy's home parish. The church is packed, not only with Wooster students, but with his high school friends as well. It is by far the youngest congregation I have ever seen at a funeral. The minister is sensitive to the situation, that almost everyone there is facing the fact of death for the first time in his or her life. He speaks poignantly and meaningfully about death, and about life. Nobody dozes.

Consider discipline.

Wells Kerr, for nearly thirty years the dean of Phillips Exeter Academy, probably expelled more boys in his career than anyone else in the entire history of American secondary education. I don't think those whom he expelled ever actually formed a club, but they might have. I know several of them, and they are a distinguished group—distinguished for their achievements in the world and by their affection for Wells Kerr. Not long ago a family sued Exeter for having expelled their son, on the grounds that the action would affect his chances in the world for the rest of his life. Exeter's legal defense was simply to point to this army of people. One became founder and first headmaster of a school (and hired Wells Kerr to teach for him after Wells's retirement from Exeter) ; another is currently a trustee of Princeton University (and named one of his sons after Wells) ; another is a distinguished judge. It has always seemed strange to me that more people in the world of education do not seem to be able to remember that the noun *discipline* comes from the same stem as the verb *to teach*. Wells Kerr was a glorious exception. Frank Boyden, of Deerfield, was another. Dr. Boyden's technique was different. It is said that during his sixty-two years as a headmaster he never once expelled a boy, though he had a way of discouraging some from continuing at Deerfield.

My most difficult problem of discipline as a headmaster has been drugs. One of my main advantages over my sons (and my students) has been the fact that I knew more about the laws of cause and effect than they did. In this area I always felt that I could teach with authority. But in the area of drugs I couldn't, and neither (in 1968 and later) could anyone else on the faculty. Early in the history of drugs at our school we decided to form a committee of both students and faculty to explore the whole question and develop some sort of code. The first meeting lasted about four hours, in the evening, and was the best discussion on the subject I have ever heard before or since. In the middle of the meeting, one boy leaned back in his chair and stretched his hands over his head. Inadvertently he touched the curtain that was closed across the window behind him. His hand felt something hard, and very quietly he said to the whole assembly, "Uh-oh! I think we're being bugged." We all looked at each other in silence, and then someone got up and went to the third floor, which was a dorm, and found and removed the bug.

Now, wasn't that a dumb thing to do! If we had gone right on with our meeting, and done nothing about the bug, there would have existed on the campus a clandestine tape of all our proceedings. What a teaching device! As it was, we spent weeks trying to convey persuasively all that had been said at the meeting to the student body as a whole. They were suspicious, and therefore not too interested. But if the information had been *illegal*, nobody would have dozed! We just didn't think fast enough.

Another disciplinary problem that I have always had difficulty dealing with is theft and vandalism. The anonymity of the crimes, of course, gets one off to a slow start. But in a close community that isn't always so bad. My experience has been that as long as the perpetrator is anonymous, the community is capable of an enormous amount of righteous indignation (one of my favorite emotions). Once the culprit is caught, the community is immediately divided. Some feel sorry for him; others admire his bravado. But as long as nobody knows who it is, much can be taught about community responsibility. Meanwhile, the guilty party knows who he is, and it is possible that it doesn't even matter whether he gets caught or not.

In the kind of school where I have spent my life, theft and vandalism usually indicate that there is some other kind of problem, that some lesson other than honesty and respect for the property of others probably needs to be taught. *Forgiveness* is the best teaching device I know in these circumstances. There is nothing like it.

Consider athletics: The jocks of this world, starting with the playing fields of Eton, or maybe the Greeks, have taken unto themselves so much credit for building the character of the young, with such boxcar loads of questionable evidence, that I hesitate to admit that there is *anything* good about competitive athletics as an educational device. But, of course, there is. I coached wrestling for ten years. I did it because I had wrestled in my youth, because it was a relatively inexpensive sport that didn't take up much space, and because at the time our school had no gym. Wrestling had done a

little something for me in terms of self-confidence, and
I liked the feature of it that you don't have to be big
to be good. There is also a lesson in the loneliness of
being out on the mat by yourself, with no one to rely
on but yourself. At the same time, wrestling is a team
sport. You are alone on the mat, but you are surrounded
by cheering friends, all cheering just for you.

Between periods in a wrestling match there is a one-
to-one relationship between the coach and the athlete
that is rare in its texture. Usually the wrestler is lying
down, the coach bending over him, wiping his forehead
with a cool, damp towel, and talking. He is, at the
moment, a combination of coach, doctor, nurse, father,
and friend.

It took a while to develop a competitive team in a
small school; so for a long time the corporate lesson
most often learned was how to lose. Finally, one day
we beat the Taft second team, and the trip home from
Watertown was hilarious. I decided that we should celebrate by having a meal on the road. We stopped at a
nice inn, but it turned out that I didn't have any
money. Somehow the proprietor found out that we had
a wrestler named Dick Burton, from around Boston.
The proprietor, who came from the same area, said,
"Not Billy Burton's boy!" To be sure, and so everyone had steak. Some days everything breaks right and
people have a chance to learn one of the more important lessons of life—what joy feels like.

Across from the entrance to Wooster School stands
an old red barn, architecturally perhaps the handsomest building on the campus, but more or less useless
except as a symbol of humble beginnings. We had a
wonderfully emotional Irishman by the name of Jack
Sullivan as a football coach, and he knew what to do
with that barn. He used it as the inner sanctum for

his pregame and between-the-halves pep talks. Jack had played at Boston College and coached at Fordham and even played a little professionally. But talking was what he did best. On Saturdays he accomplished things in that barn (I was never allowed in) that made up for all the technicalities of the game that he had failed to teach during the week. One thing was certain: Jack Sullivan never dozed, and neither did his students, which would have to indicate that he was a fine teacher —and in many ways he was.

I still feel, however, that athletics as a teaching device has one serious flaw. One year we had a Norwegian exchange student by the name of Tor Jespersen. He was six feet five and rawboned. Jack Sullivan drooled every time he looked at him. But Tor was not really interested in learning how to play football, so he just stood around until one day he became intrigued by the kickoff. He thought that was something he could do and offered to try. His first kick went over the goal line, and he was issued a uniform. That was fine, except that he wouldn't do anything else. Even on the kickoff itself, having kicked the ball, he would just stand there and watch the game from his very privileged position in the middle of the field. Jack Sullivan couldn't take it; and one day, standing beside Tor just after the kickoff, he looked up at him and said, "Thor [his own special name], after you have kicked the ball, why don't you run down the field with the rest of the team and [here he smashed the palm of his left hand with his right fist] *hit* somebody?"

Tor, looking down quizzically at his coach, said, "But why? They are no enemies of mine."

The trouble with sports as a teaching device is that there has to be an enemy. Of course, some valuable things can be taught even so, but I consider that a sizable drawback.

Death. Discipline. Athletics. All special opportunities for the docent. And then there is the unpredictable.

Every day things happen.

A girl walks by my office door. "Good morning. How are you today?"

"Fine."

"No, you're not. What's wrong?" (Anyone who lives a lifetime among the young can learn to read faces. It's not hard.)

An instant flood of tears, a desperate embrace, and between sobs: "I have a paper due this morning that I can't finish and my boyfriend has just thrown me over and I'm *having my period!*"

I was sixty years old at the time, and no female had ever before volunteered that information for me. Shall I laugh or cry? Something tells me I'd better take the whole thing very seriously. So we talk and we talk, and because neither one of us is dozing, maybe something about perspective is learned.

Now it is about ten o'clock at night and a very timid and frightened-looking boy knocks on the door of my house. His roommate is a black boy from a big-city ghetto and, says my visitor, he's just plain scared of him. "I'm afraid he's going to kill me." I don't believe that, but I know I have a problem with the young man in front of me. The problem is that it's the first week of school, he has never been away from home before, and he has never met a black boy before. Lots of talking, and finally calmness is achieved.

This time it is two o'clock in the morning and the phone rings. "Reverend, this is the Ridgefield Barracks, Officer McCarthy speaking. Reverend, we have three of your boys here, on a drug charge."

"Yes, officer. Someone will be right down. And thank you for calling."

A younger colleague is drafted to go down to the barracks and do the hand holding. I wake up our school lawyer to get a little advice and then wake up a parent who happens to be a bondsman. The boys are back before dawn, and we decide not to call the parents until a little later in the day. What the boys need is support. I don't believe in double jeopardy. They are in trouble with the law, and that is enough. They should not also be in trouble with the school or with their parents. How to persuade the parents? One father turns out to be heroic, gets the point right away, and helps us with the others. Something has been taught.

It is vacation. School is closed and nobody is around except one bachelor master; but he happens to be the real pastor of the community, living in a dorm, always available to anyone, day or night. In fact he is the very man that my friend Sam Bartlett was referring to when he gave me that sage advice, "If you find anyone in your school who can do something better than you can, get down on your knees and thank God, and let him do it." For twenty-five years, even though being a pastor was my special pride, this man, Donald G. Schwartz, did much more of a pastor's work than I because he was much better at it. The quiet of the empty dorm is disturbed by a knock on his door.

"Come in!"

In walks a very bedraggled-looking Joe Lacey, his head hung low.

"Joe, what are you doing here? Don't you know it's vacation?"

"I ran away from home."

"Let's go to Marcus and have a cup of coffee."

Marcus is the local dairy bar. It is also the unofficial confessional booth, conference center, and trysting place of the Wooster School. Two miles down the road, it is effectively part of the Wooster campus. There is no doubt that through the years Donald Schwartz has spent literally thousands of dollars on cups of coffee there. It is one place where the docent never dozes, and neither does the student. Mark Hopkins, the educator, once defined education as a teacher sitting on one end of a log and a student on the other. For years Marcus Dairy has been Wooster's log.

If education, as I understand it, cannot be fitted into a school day, or a school week, or even term time, neither can it be fitted into an arbitrary block of time marked off by matriculation and graduation. One of the most important ingredients, along with forgiveness, that it takes to guide a young person through the adolescent years is patience. But patience takes over *after* reasonableness, not as part of it. If you are waiting at the station at ten for the ten-ten, you are reasonable about it. Along about ten-fifteen or ten-twenty, when reasonableness has run out, patience should take over. The train is due, is overdue, and it isn't there. So with the end of adolescence. Under normal circumstances it takes a while. That's reasonable. But what are normal circumstances? It really doesn't matter much. All that matters is that the train eventually comes in. Sometimes about all you can do is wait patiently.

I learned this from one of my favorite students of all time, Jeremy Acheson Platt. Jeremy was a grandson of Bishop Acheson, of Connecticut, an early trustee of Wooster, and a nephew of Dean Acheson. He was a bad boy. He broke rules, he tried to get out of duties, at times he was snarly, he was very bright but didn't study, and he had a physical awkwardness that often made him less than attractive. He had a way of looking at you that completely masked what he was thinking. I was never quite sure whether I was being mocked or not.

But he had a strong personality, and beneath his adolescent ineptitudes I detected a touch of class. So I took a chance and made him a prefect during his senior year, because sometimes people who seem to be against the system really aren't and only need to be taken into the company. In any case, he went straight and did a fine job. Which is not to say that the process of his education was completed. After five years at Williams and MIT, he came back for a visit, and brought with him a bottle of Fleurie (a fine Beaujolais) and a little machine for making espresso coffee. As he produced them out of a brown paper bag, he said, "Guides to gracious living." He was at this point strikingly handsome, urbane, utterly charming, and well on his way to a brilliant career with W. R. Grace. After that visit, it suddenly occurred to me—as the truth sometimes does—that in my pride over the school where I worked, I had never considered that someone on his way to manhood might learn something somewhere else, maybe even after graduation.

Jeremy, too young, was killed in an automobile accident, and the funeral services were held in the Wooster chapel. His ashes are buried under a big rock on a hill on the edge of the woods, overlooking the dormitory that he had supervised for a year. That it is now a girls' dorm would surely delight him no end. There is a plaque on the stone that reads: "Gracious God of Good, Whose own son's term of service to mankind on earth was so full its brevity was no distress; we thank Thee now for a young life of elegance and chivalry, too brief for us but long enough for Thee. We thank Thee for

its cultured courtesy and refinement; for the beauty of
a mind light with bright imagination and precision; for
a love of people, worn not on the sleeve but in the heart;
for a morality and faith, not wholly orthodox, but
graced with the strength of sincerity and the light of
truth. We thank Thee for this young life's noble
bearing and its savoir-vivre; and we thank Thee for
the love it engendered, in the hearts of family, friends
and neighbors. Gracious God of Good, Thy will be
done. Amen."

Student lovers, walking hand in hand through the
woods, sometimes come upon it, read the words, and
wonder, Who was he? What was he? How did he get
there? That's the idea. Such wonder is a form of im-
mortality. Some people think that plaques are to help
us remember. But memory is not immortal. Wonder is.

Then there is David, to whom I shall give no last
name because he is still very much alive and well. Aca-
demically David was one of the worst students I have
ever known. During all his secondary-school years
(which were spent at several schools and many summer
schools), I don't think he ever actually passed anything. But he was just about as nice a young human as
I have ever known. Each year, at the final faculty meeting, his fate would be debated. Each year it would
be agreed that he had absolutely no academic future,
and that he really should be let go. Then someone
would say, "But how can we possibly let such a nice
guy go? We need him. Guys like that don't come along
every day. If we can't find a way to hang onto David,
and do a little something for him, then there is something wrong with us." So, we would find a way and he
would stay; until one fine day he actually received a
diploma. I have no idea how many credits he had, and
I can't even remember where he went to college. He

came to see me a few years later, looking for a little career advice. He seemed stumped because his education did not fit him into any of the neat molds of our society. On the spur of the moment I said, "David, why don't you just go out and do some good? Get a job with the Red Cross or something. They don't have people like you walking through their doors looking for work every day."

So he got a job with the Red Cross, spent several years in faraway places, doing a lot of good and a lot of thinking.

Then he came back and said, "I've decided that I want to be a hospital administrator and I've applied to Columbia. Will you write me a recommendation?" I thought of his Wooster transcript and my heart sank. With all those asterisks, indicating where this course or that course had been made up, and with what grade, it looked as though a hen with dirty feet had walked across it. And now he wanted to go to Columbia? But I said of course I would. I ended up writing something that was entirely true, entirely supportive, and that was all that needed to be said; and Columbia, to its great credit, read it right and accepted him. I wrote: "This young man can do anything he says he can do."

David has been a hospital administrator for many years, spending most of his life in very tough places, mostly in the Middle East, where he has learned to speak other languages and to get along in other cultures. He has been, in a very good sense, a kind of missionary. The United States has not had a better ambassador in that part of the world. All it took was time. No. It took more than that. But it did take time.

As proof of the pudding, independent schools have a way of flaunting their more distinguished alumni. The line of reasoning is shaky, to say the least, but the temptation is irresistible. The reason I have used the word *flaunt* is that one of its dictionary definitions is so apt: "to display ostentatiously or impudently." That was the impression I got one day when I looked at the Choate alumni magazine, which had on the cover a picture of three men—Chester Bowles, Adlai Stevenson, and John Kennedy—all graduates of Choate School. I thought that was both ostentatious and impudent, which is to say I was jealous. In terms of the size of the school and the length and quality of the list of names, Groton could probably beat everyone at this game, getting off to a fast start with Franklin Roosevelt and Dean Acheson. I have a feeling, however, that the game is becoming more and more a thing of the past. For a little bit longer into our nation's history than some of us would like to admit, there was such a thing as a kind of unofficial, but nonetheless powerful and influential, aristocracy—"the first four hundred" they used to call it when I was young. Several independent boarding schools existed and prospered more or less expressly to serve this group. It was by no means all bad. It was, in fact, rather a noble thing to be responsible for the education (intellectual and moral) of those who were "destined" to be our country's leaders. The model, of course, was English. Eton, Harrow, and Rugby set the pace; and it was natural to think that the process could be duplicated in America. I have no quarrel with the attempt at all; I think there were instances of great good coming from it. But essentially the idea is not American, as Exeter, Andover, Mount Hermon, and other schools decided early on and as almost everyone in the field realizes today. The result is that the American independent school is much more American than it used to be.

What bothered me about the flaunting, apart from

jealousy, was the implication that this or that success story was evidence that a good educational job was being done. If so, the failures should be "flaunted" too. On my only visit to Eton, I remember being struck by the oppressiveness of the success story, as displayed by plaques and lists and portraits all over the place. How could a fifteen-year-old boy *ever* be right and the school *ever* be wrong? An institution that simply has to be right all the time is a tough place for a young person to grow up in.

The point is that in the education of adolescents, no one ever knows for sure whether he has done well, even whether he has done good. Sometimes alumni write nice letters saying nice things. When they send their children to you, you are tempted to think that you must have done something right when they were in school. But it could be sheer sentimentality, merely a father making his son after his own image. In talking to young people who want to be teachers, I always tell them to forget the whole thing if they are looking for gratitude. They will rarely be thanked and, when they are, will not be sure what for. Probably that is a good thing.

Having made my apologies, I must close this chapter by flaunting one of the graduates of the school where I have spent my life.

Peter Jason Fine was graduated from Wooster in 1953. He became a doctor, lost his hearing as the result of a brain tumor, learned sign language and lip reading, became the physician for Gallaudet College (for the deaf) for five years, and died in 1975. Testimony to the significance of his life work was provided at his funeral service, in a church packed with young and old, black and white, Catholic, Protestant, and Jew, some hearing and some deaf. The whole service, in which many people took part, was signed by a Catholic priest, a close friend.

At Wooster, Peter had done everything well except play football. He was big and strong and handsome and an exceptionally fast runner. The only trouble was that he ran mostly sideways and backwards. At the time the coach thought he was afraid. It is a shame that the coach did not live long enough to learn that Peter Fine was the most courageous young man he had ever coached in his life. He just happened to have been born gentle and shared some of the feelings of our young Norwegian boy about enemies.

Peter was an actor, with a fine singing voice. He was also a good student, and a leader. He was the first Jew to be made a prefect in the school's history. He was the kind of schoolboy that one would expect to be a "success in life." But there would have been no way to predict the courage with which he fought his illness, and the incredible drive that enabled him to carve out a whole new career after he became deaf, or the sensitivity with which he tried not to inflict his handicap on others. Before he died, he wrote the following letter to my wife and me:

Dear John and Sue,

I am suddenly moved to write to you because of the fact that I must once more go into the hospital, this time on January 1, for surgery on my head. It seems the left-sided tumor has returned and is much larger than the first time and that I've a second one, something new, in my neck. I was to have gone in yesterday, but my doctor said that I will get better care after the Christmas holidays.

This letter is not prompted by anxiety or fear, because, strangely enough, I have none. . . . All this began about four months ago when swallowing became a little difficult. Since then it has become more so, my voice is nearly gone due to a left-sided vocal cord paralysis, and my left shoulder is weakened. The tests showed a "huge tumor in the left cerebellopontine angle," which translates into a big mess causing a larger mess.

Perhaps it is not appropriate for me to write this to you at this time of the year with the joys of Christmas approaching, but you, my old friends, I wanted to know. The odds this time for survival are fifty-fifty, but then again Perry Black, my close friend and neurosurgeon, said the same thing last time. There are so many reactions I could have—anger, resentment, fear, frustration—but they are all absent. Perhaps you taught me something at Wooster after all. The Lord works in strange ways, and who am I to question him? . . .

All in all, it has been a good year. My work is enjoyable and has afforded me many new friends, all of whom are worried sick. . . . We had a superb vacation in Jamaica this summer but will not go back because the poverty is so depressing.

Sorry to be the giver of bad news, but I am and will always be grateful to you for imparting so much faith to me. Perhaps that explains why I am at peace with myself and the world.

Have a joyous Christmas and Happy New Year.

Godbless,

Peter

John, I'm sure I need not ask, but please say a prayer for me.

Shortly after his death, Marcia Glick, a student at Gallaudet College and a patient of Peter's, wrote the following for the Gallaudet College paper.

What does it mean to be deaf? We, each of us, have our stories, and so our definitions will vary, depending on experience. If I say I am deaf, am I less of a person? Am I not capable of functioning at whatever level I consider to be most satisfying? Have I not the right to make my life what I will?

I knew a man, a very wonderful person. Dr. Peter Jason Fine passed away on the 20th of this month [September 1975], and I have lost my good friend. We have all suffered a great loss.

Come, let us sit around and trade Dr. Fine stories. Mine will live in my memory as long as I exist, and I am totally grateful for the gift of having known him.

I first met Dr. Fine when I reported to the infirmary as a new student, although I had known a bit about him before. A deaf friend had told me about Gallaudet's unique physician. A deaf man practicing medicine. Wow! Not to be believed, at least not within the realm of my experience. . . .

I sit across from him in his office. He begins signing and finger-spelling a mile a minute until I tell him I do not understand. I am frightened, he knows it. I do not know how to sign and, like him, I also became deaf.

"So you'll learn, and if I could learn it, so will you. *Zol Zein mit glück*," he spelled slowly. My last name means luck in Yiddish and German, and Doc was telling me "good luck" while playing on my name. He was telling me much more actually,

by his use of the Jewish language idiom, for he
was telling me, in non-verbal ways, that he was
familiar with my culture.

So many times when we met, he would tease me
with Jewish expressions and New York slang,
and as I sit here writing this, again I am filled with
the happy warmth that came from his kindness.
He was a fine doctor, a humorous and warm person who cared very much about people.

Dr. Fine became deaf as a result of neurosur-
gery for brain tumors, his first bout with that bit-
terest of forces that ultimately claimed him. I do
not know what he was like before his illness. It
would appear that he had had the promise of success as a young physician, and along came fate
and slapped him a stunning blow.

Can a deaf man practice medicine? Can a deaf
person be a computer programmer or a lawyer, a
designer, a reporter or a teacher? Yes, yes, yes,
we can be what we are capable of, and we are capable of almost any number of different things. And
how do I know this? I have met many hearing-
impaired people occupying all manner of professional roles, and I knew Peter Fine, a deaf man who
practiced medicine, and Dr. Fine drummed home
that lesson. He was a man with a sense of worth,
true to himself. . . .

A stethoscope lies atop a cabinet, useless and
ignored. His hands, his sensitive hands!

"You eat too much. You smoke too much. You
never sleep like normal people do and your ear
is infected, but otherwise you'll live. Everything
I say to you falls on deaf ears, right?" And he
puts drops into my hurting ear, placing his other
hand on my other ear as if to catch the drops fall-

ing through my head, for he has told me there is
absolutely nothing at all but empty space between
my two ears. I loved him.

We sat in his office, chatting about everything
and anything. I told him of noise in my head from
tinnitus and that I always hear music. He looks
far away for a minute and sighs. I look at him
closely. We each know what is going on in the
other's mind. He says, his expression as open and
wistful as mine, "Oh, you're lucky to be able to
hear it, even from memory. I miss music so much.
That is the one thing that really hurts. Not to be
able to hear it again." A shared pain. He loved the
classics, he told me, and once wanted to be a con-
cert violinist. The moment was over, for you cannot dwell on what you cannot have.

The last time I saw Dr. Fine was in December
(1974) in the Abbey. It was final exam week and
I had been nearly without sleep for most of the
week in a last-ditch attempt to cram five courses'
worth of learning into the minute capacity of my
head. It was morning and as I sat there downing
cup after cup of coffee, he entered and came over
and said . . .

"Nu efsha?" (Well, what's with you?)

"Doc," I replied, "I'm dying!"

"Yeah, is that so? So am I."

Suddenly wide awake, I felt so cold, freezing
cold, with the growing awareness of what I was
about to be told. I looked at him closely. The gen-
tlest of expressions upon his face, he told me he
was sick again with only a fifty percent chance of
survival. . . .

Twice in my life I have visited Wooster alumni in their prison cells, where each had been incarcerated for good and sufficient reason. It did not occur to me that it was my fault that they were there. So, I take no credit for Peter Fine. I could be wrong on both counts, or either count. I'll never know. Peter Fine is not an example of the kind of person we turn out in our school; his life is merely a supreme example of what we hope and pray for. I do think it is safe to say that when Peter was a student, at Wooster and before and after, he didn't doze much; and when he became a docent, he didn't doze much either. And that's what education is . . . and was.

A Second Country

O NE blisteringly hot July afternoon during a summer vacation I found myself standing in the
chancel of the Roman Catholic church in a small village
in the south of France, looking out at the congregation.
It was a funeral service. The closed coffin lay before the
altar. The priest was introducing me and explaining
to the people who I was and why I was there. Since it
was a mission parish which this priest served only occasionally, and since my family and I had lived in that
village for an entire year fifteen years before, and
since a number of those present never darkened the
door of the church except for such special occasions, it
would not have been entirely inappropriate for me to
have been introducing him. But the situation was unusual enough as it was, particularly when he couldn't
remember the name of the town in the United States
where I came from and someone in the congregation
volunteered the information.

As the priest spoke, my eyes roamed over the faces

of my friends and acquaintances. They turned first to the new widow and caught her tearful eye and sad, but warm, smile. I was there because she had asked me. Two weeks before, on the night of the feast of St. Jean, she had invited me and another friend from the village named Jean (which was also her husband's name), with our wives, to celebrate our common saint's day together. It was a gay occasion, during which we three Jeans drank to the health of our wives, and indirectly to our own with the addition to the toast of the Provençal fillip, "May they never be widows." Now, suddenly, one of them was. She had called from Paris, where her Jean had died, to say that the funeral service would be in the village church and the burial in the local cemetery and that I must take part in the service. Although it was the first time in my life that I had taken part in a Roman Catholic service in a Roman Catholic church, and the first time I had taken part in a church service of any kind in France, of course I accepted. Her smile was her thanks.

As the priest spoke on, my eyes roamed some more. There was the other Jean, one of my closest friends in France. He is a retired stonemason, small but as rugged as the rocks he has spent his life splitting. His strength showed in his face just then, in his eyes, in the muscles of his jaw, and in the corners of his mouth, turned up a little, but not in a smile. Next to him was his wife, Germaine, one of Suzanne's closest friends in France. I thought how rare such totally congenial foursomes are, and I remembered our initial meeting, fifteen years before, when we had first arrived in that village with four small children, speaking virtually no French. Then it was the strength of Jean's arms and back that had impressed me. The path to our house was too narrow for even a small truck, so Jean, who is not much more than half my size, simply lifted each of our trunks on his shoulders and carried them up the hill, one after the other. And Germaine started immediately to give Sue lessons in how to get along in a rather rudimentary Provençal kitchen, where to buy food, what to buy, and how to take care of old tile floors.

There were many others in the church whom I knew: the wife of the *garagiste*, the mayor, and Monsieur Rey, a retired electrician who had shown me during our first week in the village how to fix a French fuse without having to buy a new one. He was the first Communist I had ever met.

As I looked around the church itself, I remembered the first time we had worshipped there at a Christmas Eve midnight service. On this stifling July afternoon the sweat was pouring down my face, but I could remember how cold it had been that night and how ineffectual the potbellied, wood-burning stove that sat in the middle of the center aisle had been. And I remembered how miserable our whole family had been that night, suffering from a violent attack of homesickness, and how we had recovered, thanks to the warmth and understanding of our friends and neighbors, the very people before me now.

I was brought back to the present by the sudden realization that the priest was about to finish his remarks about me (which he did with the charmingly ecumenical and shockingly unorthodox statement, "He is as much a priest as I am"). It was my turn to step forward and offer a prayer. I opened my arms, as I always do at such a moment, and said, *"Seigneur soit avec vous."* The response came back, *"Et avec votre esprit."* In English I have said those words and received that response literally thousands of times in my life. "The Lord be with you." "And with thy spirit." I have never taken the exchange casually, but I think it has never been more meaningful to me than it was at that moment.

When I had finished my prayer, the priest conducted the rest of the service, and at the end he took the aspergillum and sprinkled holy water on the coffin three times, in the name of the Father and the Son and the Holy Ghost, then turned and, to my utter astonishment, handed it to me to repeat what he had done.

There were no honorary pallbearers, no smoothly rolling chariot. As we left the church, my friend Jean and five other men lifted the coffin by its six handles and carried it out. Later they lowered it into the grave by the strength of their own backs—no machines. The women picked up the flowers from the altar and carried them to the cemetery. We followed the hearse through the village in a silent procession such as my wife and I had witnessed any number of times as tourists, in any number of French villages, never dreaming that one day we would be in such a procession ourselves, belonging, following a neighbor to his grave.

A friend of mine, who had traveled a good deal and lived abroad on more than one occasion, used to say to Sue and me, over and over again, as we were in the process of falling in love with France, "Everyone should have a second country. . . . Mine is Greece." Ours is France.

For a great many Americans, including several of our personal friends, America is itself their second country. That's a different matter. I speak here not of change of citizenship, and definitely not of expatriation. I speak of a special kind of haven, to which one can repair now and then, from which one can regain perspective about home and job and friends and causes and ideas and ideals. If one lives and works in New York

City, as E. B. White did for so many years, one can always go to Maine from time to time, as he did—to his benefit and to the benefit of all of us who read him. Surely Maine has meant to him and his family many of the same things that France has meant to me and my family. But maybe that is just a way of saying that from New York City, Maine is a second country. They speak a different language there, follow different customs, live by a different style, and laugh and worry about different things.

Sue's and my affair with France started with our going there as tourists. We had decided on France, rather than some other country, more or less by chance, like a blind date. We made all the stupid tourist mistakes, came home after our first three-week trip authorities on France and "the French," and bored our friends with endless anecdotes and pictures. But as we and our blind date got better and better acquainted, the affair became more and more serious.

In 1963 I had a year's sabbatical leave from Wooster, by which time it was a foregone conclusion that we would spend it in France. The village where the funeral took place was our home for that year. The population of the village at that time was sixty people, and as we were a family of six, we were immediately ten percent of the town's inhabitants. None of us spoke French, and no one in the village spoke English. The night of our arrival we were frightened at what we had done, homesick and so lonely that we all cried over breakfast and tried to figure out how we could call the whole thing off and go home. A year later, our car packed to the roof and beyond, surrounded by our village friends, the children's schoolmates included, we all cried again because we *had* to go home.

Between those tearful occasions, two of our sons,

aged seven and eleven, had attended the village school, and our oldest son, then fourteen, had attended a boarding school two hundred kilometers away. I was so impressed with the effects of this experience, especially for our oldest son, that upon our return to Wooster I suggested a program for sending students to France for a year of study and of living with a French family in Provence. By 1980 more than 130 students had been on that program, Sue and I having visited and selected all of the families and having each year given a dinner in their honor. Twice the United States ambassador has come from Paris to attend the dinners. At one dinner, thanks to the kind offices of my French friends, I was decorated by the French government. I have always made a speech at these affairs in French; and each year one of the students has assigned himself to keep track of the number of grammatical mistakes I make—and report to me. In 1972 that self-appointed student-teacher was my own son. The score was five mistakes in a twenty-minute talk, a record for me at the time.

In 1968 we took the whole family to France again for the summer, first renting a house in a village not very far from the one where we had spent our year. At the end of the summer, our landlord announced that he was selling the house and asked if we wanted to buy it. We had been looking and talking within the family, but now the issue had been dumped in our laps. There were no nay votes. The house was bought, and in it my wife and daughter and I have spent every summer since, as well as several spring vacations. We have not yet all been back again together, and maybe we never shall be. But each son has been back several times, sometimes with a girl friend and, as they married, with wives.

That blind date with France has become a serious affair. We have a second country.

In his book *Adaptation to Life* (Little, Brown, 1977), Dr. George Vaillant evaluates the lives of some of the subjects of what has come to be known as the Grant Study. This study started in 1939 with the selection of 268 promising young men whose lives were then followed in great detail for thirty-five years by a team of highly trained specialists. The goal was to try to determine what factors make for a healthy life, healthy from every imaginable standpoint—family life, business or professional success, friendships, as well as reasonable physical and mental health. A theme that runs constantly through Dr. Vaillant's book is that the ability to relax, to play, to take meaningful vacations, is the one thing that all the healthiest of the men he interviewed at the end of the thirty-five years seemed to have in common.

I was not a part of that study, though I am exactly the same age as many of those who were. Also, I have never "been studied," so I have no objective basis for judging my healthiness. But I do think that I am blessed with the ability to have fun, to relax; and long before I discovered a second country, I knew how to benefit from a vacation. All vacations should provide rest and relaxation, a change of pace, some new perspective, and most important of all, some new enthusiasm for going back to work. For years I have had to put up with the scoffing of my friends in the business world about the length of vacations in my world. It has never bothered my conscience, given the length of the workday in my profession and the fact that there are seven of these each week. Those long vacations are not deserved, not earned. They are needed, if throughout the school year the docent is not to doze. I am not sur-

prised by the findings of the Grant Study. Without
exception, the best teachers I have known have been
the ones who best knew what to do with themselves when
they were not teaching, who knew how to relax. I used
to do my relaxing on Cape Cod. Now I do it in France,
and it seems a little better to me.

When I leave my job for vacation and twenty-four
hours later find myself in my village in Provence, my
head clears and my muscles relax somewhat more completely than they did when I got off the train at Hyan-
nis to be met by my bronzed family, after having sorted
them out from the waiting army of other bronzed families. The people we meet during our first stroll down
the village street do not know what has happened in
our lives since last we saw each other, any more than
we know what has happened in theirs. And that is good.
Our working worlds are different, and so we talk about
something else, for us in a different language. And
that, too, is good. We have one neighbor who greets us,
not only when we have just returned from the States,
but every time he sees us, with *"Ahhh, les américains,
toujours en vacances!"* We all laugh. Because I have
the kind of job that follows me around to a certain
extent (there is nothing contradictory about working
while vacationing), he is not quite right. I work every
day. But in another sense he is absolutely right. Whenever I am in France, I am *en vacances*, and so is my
wife.

Part of the explanation lies, perhaps, in being on
vacation, not just from my job and my surroundings,
but from myself. I am someone else in France, someone I
find rather refreshing. My wife also finds my French
self refreshing. After three days she invariably says,
"You're beginning to lose the sacks under your eyes."

Psychiatrists speak of the identity crisis as a disturbance caused by not knowing exactly who you are. For me the contrary is true. I know very well who I am and sometimes get a little tired of the daily identity with whom I have to live and work.

When we first arrived in our little village on my sabbatical, I was obsessed with the idea of anonymity. I had not yet worked out my theory of a different self, but instinctively I knew that part of the purpose of a sabbatical was to give me a rest from the role of headmaster-priest. I didn't want people to know what I did for a living, so much so that I got quite angry with my son Daniel one evening when he came home from the café (where he had been learning French in his own way) and said, "You know, Dad, they think you're a pretty big man in this town." Immediately I bristled. "Daniel, you haven't been talking too much, have you?" "No, I haven't said a thing! They just mean that you're taller than most of the other men in the village." I needn't have worried. Nobody asked me about myself, and if anyone had I would have had trouble explaining, because I didn't know the French word for *headmaster*. I have since learned that the word is *proviseur*, which in the thirteenth century, according to my etymological dictionary, was defined as *fournisseur*, which means, among other things, "caterer." I find that information absolutely delightful and share it with any headmaster I meet who seems to be taking himself and his position too seriously. And maybe that's why the French people of our village didn't take me too seriously. My real identity for them was as Sue's husband and my children's father, an American who had entrusted two of his children to the local school, whose activity during the working part of the day was unknown but probably not very interesting, and who was trying to learn to speak French, to play *boules* and *belote*, and to drink *pastis*.

Two minor incidents might have upset the apple cart but didn't. During the year I was asked to consider the possibility of becoming headmaster of another school, one of whose trustees was a member of President Johnson's White House staff. This man wrote me two letters, sent in envelopes engraved *The White House, Washington, D.C.* Monsieur Rolly, the postmaster, could not read English, but he did manage to decipher those words, and for a short time I lived in fear that our neighbors might become suspicious about just who we were. There was no sign of special interest.

The other incident was caused by a photograph in our school newspaper, which happened to be lying on the kitchen table when our friend Germaine came to call. I had received an honorary degree from Princeton just before leaving for France, and the picture was of me in all my glad rags being hooded. Germaine picked up the paper, took one look, then looked at me, pulled her skirt out sideways with the thumb and forefinger of each hand, curtsied, and said, *"Majesté!"* We all laughed, and that is what she has called me ever since. One can lose one's identity in a second country.

Well and good for me, but what about my wife? Isn't housekeeping, housekeeping; and cooking three meals a day, cooking three meals a day; and washing dishes, washing dishes; whether in America or in France? Yes and no, but that first year, far more no. There were no supermarkets then, and no frozen foods. There was still a separate store for everything; one for bread, another for meats, and another for vegetables—at least when we went into the nearest big town for major shopping. Something that always delighted me was that every time Sue came out of a shop, with her heavy-laden basket over her arm, she had a smile on her face and couldn't wait to tell what had happened. There was always an incident, or a bit of conversation, and usually it was pleasant.

One day some American friends were going to stop by for a meal and Sue decided to serve pigeons. We were told that we could buy them from Madame Valentine, who had a farm outside the village. There we went, and were surprised by a lot of things. First, the farm, which was not so very small, was run entirely by this one lady and her mother, aged about sixty and eighty respectively. Second, we couldn't buy the pigeons without first sitting with the mother and daughter in the kitchen and sampling their homemade liqueur. Third, we noticed that the mother sat in the corner with her hands folded in her lap, not uttering a word and not seeming to pay any attention. We assumed that she was deaf; but after a while her daughter apologized and explained that her mother didn't speak French! In response to our look of surprise, she added that her mother spoke only Provençal, an ancient language that, in spite of the noble efforts of the poet Frédéric Mistral, early in this century, was fast dying out. And fourth, and finally, when the pigeons were handed to us, they were alive!

Since neither one of us had ever killed a bird or plucked one, Sue's friend Germaine had to come to the rescue. She quickly grabbed two of the birds by the head, one in each hand, and twirled them in a circle, one clockwise and the other counterclockwise, put them down, dead, and grabbed two more. Then she began to pluck, singing, "*Alouette, gentille alouette. Alouette, je te plumerai.*" It is a Canadian song, but she knew it. While she was busy singing and plucking, one of the birds lying on the table moved a little. With no lost motion, and hardly looking up, she grabbed it as before and gave it another twist. My American housewife was still a housewife in France, but her identity, like mine, took on a new dimension.

Now, fifteen years later, things have changed a lot. There are supermarkets, and they are disgustingly like the ones at home, including the canned music, interrupted regularly by the announcement of some special bargain on counter so-and-so. Sue hardly ever comes out of these smiling, and there are seldom incidents to report, and no conversation. On the other hand, the fish man still comes to our village every Tuesday at ten and blows his horn, and my wife joins the other wives in the village to make her purchase and to exchange gossip. From this expedition she usually does return smiling.

And there is still market day! Saturday in Apt, Sunday in L'Isle-sur-Sorgue, and Monday in Cavaillon. At home I hardly ever go shopping with my wife, but in France, like many of our neighbors, we go as a family. It's an outing. We wander through the colorful crowds, brushing elbows with all sorts and conditions of men and women and children, listening to the hawkers hawk, examining the quality of the tomatoes here and the olives there, noting what is just coming in season and what is fading out. Frozen foods have come to France, but they are still not very plentiful in our area and not part of market day. So we experience, as we did in our youth at home, sadness because the strawberries are ending and joy because the melons are coming into their own.

We like the market day at L'Isle-sur-Sorgue the best. Since it is on Sunday, all the Moroccan and Algerian field hands are there, buying live chickens and carrying them off by their feet. Sometimes one hears almost as much Arabic as French. Everyone is dressed up—not formally, but colorfully. Everything shuts down suddenly at exactly twelve o'clock, and we find a café in the shade and have a *pastis* before returning to our village.

Whether one is a housewife or a headmaster at home, one finds in a second country that one is a slightly different self. And that is good.

In our second country, not only are we different people, but we must speak a different language. In spite of the fact that both Sue and I had to learn this different language when we were rather old for that sort of thing, this has been one of the attractions of our second country. One speaks of a *language barrier,* and surely such a thing exists between two people with different mother tongues. As a friend of mine who was born French but has lived in America as a naturalized American citizen for the past thirty years said to me recently, "No one is bilingual." It is well known, indeed, that language can be a barrier even between two people with the same mother tongue. "England and America are two great nations," wrote George Bernard Shaw, "separated by a common language."

But language can also be a bond. "We speak the same language," one says of a special friend. Or, as the Quakers say, "He speaks to my condition." For us the French language is both a barrier and a bond.

The barrier consists partly of the simple fact that we have a limited vocabulary and make mistakes. In our early days I told a neighbor that I had just been to an *exhibition* of an artist that we both knew. He burst out laughing, partly because that word in French connotes a certain indecency and partly because the show itself (which he had also seen) was rather indecent; and

I learned that the word for an art show is *exposition*. One day when Sue was going to town, Germaine asked her if she would bring her back *un peigne*, so Sue thought. She, therefore, returned from her shopping with a new comb for her friend. Unfortunately, that left Germaine and Jean a little hungry at night because what she really wanted was a loaf of bread; she had said *pain*, with a thick Provençal accent.

Another time, when we returned from a trip during which we had left our two youngest sons in Germaine's care, she told us, among other things, that Donald's bicycle, a very old secondhand item that we had bought from a man down the street, had died. If we had been more discerning, we would have become suspicious of her surprise at how calmly we took this news. Then the next day, as a solemn funeral procession passed by the house, just like the one we were to take part in fifteen years later, including many of the same people, we realized that it was *the man who had sold us the bicycle who had died!*

One winter evening a woman showed up at our door to pay a call on behalf of a mutual friend. She stayed about four hours and talked incessantly and rapidly, leaving us exhausted. That night, for the first time in my life, I dreamed in French. When I reported this unusual experience the next morning at breakfast, son Donald said, "Could you understand it?"

In addition to the misunderstandings and embarrassments of communicating in a not thoroughly mastered second language, there is the frustration of not being able to say exactly what you want to say. The reason I could eventually make a speech in French with only five mistakes is that I was careful to say what I *knew how* to say, rather than necessarily just what I *wanted* to say. The chairman of Wooster's Modern Language Department, as fine a linguist as I know, says everybody does that, which is perhaps what my naturalized friend meant when he said that nobody is completely bilingual.

I made up my mind early on that I was not going to waste my time learning the subjunctive. (The only exception is *"Seigneur soit avec vous."*) Anything requiring the subjunctive just wouldn't get said by me. In my case, it has proved to be a marvelous discipline; not being able to say what I think, occasionally I say nothing, because, if expressing a particular thought is a struggle, one thinks twice about whether or not the thought is worth expressing at all. My family and many of my friends think it would be a great thing if some way could be found to force this question on me more often in my mother tongue. I love to talk!

As I have said, if the French language is for us a barrier, it is also a bond. In fact, the barrier itself is a bond. Most of the French people we know either don't speak English at all or speak it so little that we are better off in French. They are proud of their language and pleased with anyone who tries to speak it, however haltingly. They are all French teachers at heart, making corrections unhesitatingly, assuming that you want them to, but also showering you with praise for the least little sign that something has been learned. My daughter took a few French lessons some years ago from the daughter of Madame Albertini, who runs the *épicerie* in our present village. One day as we walked past while she was standing in the doorway, she said, *"Bonjour. Ça va?"* with the normal emphasis on the last word and the inflection of a question. My daughter replied, *"Ça va!"* with exactly the right emphasis on the first word and the drop in her voice on the second word to indicate a statement. "*Ahhh*," said Madame Albertini, "*on fait beaucoup de progrès!*" It wasn't much, but it was a bond.

Just as the speaker of a foreign tongue must give special thought and attention to what he is saying, so the native listener must give special attention and make a special effort to understand. Such attention and such an effort are flattering and friendly. Frustrating as it sometimes is for me to speak French, I love to do it because people listen so carefully. By contrast, words so often cheaply said in one's mother tongue are as often received with the cheap attention that they deserve.

Activity, of course, leads to communication, which leads to language learning. The tourist in France first learns restaurant, hotel, and highway French. Living in our village on sabbatical, we learned housekeeping French and maintenance-and-repair French. Through the Wooster program, we began to learn educational French. And as homeowners, we learned real estate French and neighborly French. I don't really blame language teachers for handing out vocabulary lists; they really have no choice. But words are not just black ink marks on white paper; they are symbols of realities. The word *ramonage*, for example, means "chimney sweeping"—in our part of France, still very much a part of everyday life. If you have a fire, before you can collect your insurance, you have to prove that you had had your chimney swept within the preceding twelve months. And *la police* means not only the police, but the insurance policy.

When there is a *mistral*, that famous wind that descends into Provence down the Rhône valley, carrying the cold air of the northern Alps, it immediately becomes a factor in community life. It starts about ten in the morning and blows until about ten at night. It moans and it howls and it whistles and it gusts. It blows dirt through the house and sometimes the plaster off the walls; in summer, it dries one's skin, and in winter, penetrates one's bones. Once it blew the bolted gate of our terrace open, and I found a small piece of the gate, with the bolt attached, about twenty feet away. The *mistral* is hard to walk against and impossible to talk against. But it becomes the one thing everyone talks about. *"Oh, c'est penible!" "Oui, c'est penible."* From the *mistral* I learned the full meaning of the word *penible*. Anybody who has studied any French at all knows that it means "painful." But the dictionary says it means "laborious, hard, irksome, heavy, stiff, arduous, rough, painful, distressing, sad, trying, severe, unpleasant" . . . like three or four days of the *mistral*.

Along with our separate identities in France and our love of the language, the third factor that makes our second country meaningful to us is the people. I don't mean "the French," because, of course, we have learned that there is no such thing, and that the phrase has certain insulting implications to anyone who is French. I mean, simply, our friends and acquaintances who are French. Like our friends and acquaintances at home, they are part of our lives, an added dimension. It is they who make us feel at home in our second country.

Because of the Wooster program, we have had the good fortune to become reasonably well acquainted with well over one hundred families. Some of them have become friends, and a few of them very close friends. The list includes the families of plumbers, stonemasons, doctors, school principals, surgeons, postmasters, farmers, atomic scientists, restaurateurs, shopkeepers, teachers, and one editor of a fashion magazine. We have dined in the homes of many of them; have been offered the use of the seaside cottages of two of them; and we *tutoyer* at least a dozen of them, including the mayor of the village where we live. Among them all are three couples whose relationship with my wife and me, and indeed with our children, has a special texture that has enriched our lives to an extraordinary extent. In all three cases the friendship is evenly distributed among husbands and wives.

André and Simone are about ten years younger than we. He is a school principal and the director of our program. Because we are thrown together professionally, it is natural that we should see one another often; but we have developed a relationship that goes beyond that in intimacy. In the course of school business, Sue and I have many times spent the night in their home, and once they spent two weeks with us in the United States. Their oldest daughter spent a year at Wooster and many evenings with us at that time. André is the gourmet *par excellence*. He knows how to cook and how to eat and how to appreciate good food and wine. He is the one who teases me the most about my French, correcting my faults as though I were one of his less able students. Of all the French people I know in the world of education, I think he understands best the nature of the teen-age psyche.

Each year in the spring, André, Suzanne, and I visit families who have expressed interest in having an American student. Inevitably the conversations follow a pattern. The same questions come up time and time again, and the answers are always the same. Through the years, the operation has developed into something that almost seems a carefully rehearsed play, in which each of the three of us has a definite role. Sue plays mother, visits the room where the student will sleep, comments favorably (at least until we get outside), and persuades the French housewife by her feminine presence that these two men are really all right. André lectures on all aspects of health, education, and welfare, while rolling himself one cigarette after another. I sit with my white hair, trying to look wise and wonderful and just. The big problem for all of us is to keep a straight face.

With deep concern a mother asks, "What about diet?" She is being asked to take on an American teenager in her own home for a year, and it is a fair question. She leans a little forward in her chair to emphasize the intensity of her interest in the answer. "Ah!" says the father, to indicate that he is interested, too. What neither of them knows is that they are the 120th family to ask that question and that André has inevitably developed a set answer. It happens to include a warning against serving rabbit the first day and the suggestion that when they do, *"Dites pas la couleur"* ("Don't say what it is") for at least twenty-four hours, "because in America they don't eat rabbit, any more than we eat cats." We have been teasing André for years about the speech on the grounds that it is not true that we don't eat rabbit and that he makes it sound as though we do eat cats. So how do we keep from laughing in front of these nice people as André launches into his routine?

Simone generally does not accompany us on our family visiting, but when she does her observations are shrewd. Once, as we were walking back to our car after a particularly congenial visit in a very beautiful home, having been plied with *pastis* and charming conversation, she said, "I found those people delightful; but if I were a teen-ager, living with them for a year, I don't think I would." On her hunch the family was not chosen. Like her husband, Simone is a fine cook, though she gets most of her gourmet pleasure from watching others eat. She is also a designer of store-window displays and, among close friends, sometimes reveals an extraordinary talent as a comedienne. With her experience as the mother of two daughters, together with a natural talent with the young, she is invaluable to the program. In spite of the difference in their ages, she and Sue enjoy each other's company like a couple of college roommates off on a spree.

There have already been several references to Jean and Germaine, to which perhaps only one vignette need be added. It has to do with the relationship between Jean and me. The contrast in our backgrounds is striking. Jean, who is ten years older than I, quit school when he was twelve, reads and writes hardly at all, but can calculate square meters in his head and knows everything there is to know about his natural surroundings. Physically, he is a tough person, with a gallantry toward females similar to my grandfather's and a disarming ability to laugh, to get angry, and to sulk. He speaks a little Italian and a lot of Provençal, as well as French. He has a slightly philosophical turn of mind and is a storehouse of proverbs. When we meet for the first time each year, he embraces me and, as he often needs a shave, practically takes the skin off my cheek with his beard.

One beautiful summer Sunday, off on one of our annual summer outings in the mountains, Jean and I went for a long walk together while our wives fixed a picnic lunch. We were on top of the world, with wheat fields and vineyards beneath us, other mountains off in the distance, and blue sky and soft clouds and bright sun over us. As we walked, Jean talked. He stopped to examine a small wild flower and tell me about it. He studied the ground for wild boar tracks. He pointed to a place where he had found some truffles the year before. He indicated a barn in the valley where he had hid during the Resistance. Finally, we sat down under a huge oak tree and he carried on for half an hour. There I was, with my college education, my graduate study, my honorary degrees, sitting at the feet of a master, asking the questions. I don't really remember what all the conversation was about; I only know that I have seldom felt closer to a human than I did to him that day.

Pierre and Micheline are very different. Pierre is a doctor in a neighboring town, as was his father and as is his son; and Micheline, though not a doctor, did study medicine and met her husband in medical school. Our youngest son, Benjamin, lived with them in the Wooster French program for a year. Between Micheline and my wife is the bond that they have shared a son. But beyond that they are just naturally *sympa*, as they say in Provence. They have many interests in common; they are outraged by the same things and are amused by the same things. They both manage their husbands' lives, giving their husbands the impression that they don't. They both know how to entertain in style. On the other hand, Micheline loves to play cards and was once president of the Parent-Teachers Association in her town. Neither of these are things my wife would ever be likely to become involved with, which gives the friendship some contrasts. Back in America, whenever Sue goes to the hairdresser, she whiles away the time under the dryer writing to Micheline, in French. Micheline is greatly amused by the fact that she can keep track of the condition of Sue's hair all winter long through this correspondence. She writes back in English, though when the two are together, they invariably speak French.

In contrast to my friend Jean, Pierre's formal education, intellectual knowledge, and general cultural background are superior to mine. He is the kind of family doctor and shrewd human psychologist that is fast fading from the American medical scene. Although we had known each other long before, our intimate friendship was launched by his deep affection for my son and his profound understanding of him. When we are together, Pierre and I talk of many things and agree on most things; but our strongest bond is laughter. Like me, he is a mimic; he is also witty, and quick, and he adores the absurd. The first time the four of us were together after Benjamin started living with them, my son confessed to having anticipated our visit with considerable apprehension, to foreseeing a contest looming between his two fathers for the center of the stage and for laughs. Wanting to be loyal to me, he nevertheless said, "I don't know, Dad. He may be too much for you." When the doctor ended the evening standing on the dining-room table, with his pants rolled up over his knees, wearing a bread basket for a hat, doing an impression of someone or other (all on only one glass of wine), I knew my best chance for survival was to play the straight man.

One day, when Pierre was going to make a speech at a medical convention, he asked me if I knew any medical jokes. I knew several and proceeded to tell them, which, incidentally, was a new type of test for my linguistic ability. Each time he got the point instantly and burst out laughing. (Like mine, his laugh is a kind of childish giggle.) Then he would be silent for a few minutes, thinking, and then retell my joke in good French, often acting it out.

One story was about a fellow who had flunked out of

medical school but couldn't bear the disgrace back home. So he bought himself a black bag and went home and hung up his shingle. He didn't know anything about medicine. His first patient arrived in the office with some rare disease and the "doctor" proceeded to examine him at length. Finally, he put down his stethoscope, looked at the patient, and said, in deadly seriousness, "Have you ever had this before?" "Oh, yes," said the patient, to which the "doctor" replied, "Well, you've got it again." That is what is known as a dumb joke. But Pierre laughed. Our two sons, his son and Benjamin, were in the room at the time, and for the next hour Pierre retold that dumb joke about twenty times, interspersed with silences while he thought of news ways of embellishing it. It ended up as a one-act play, Pierre playing both parts, to the delight of his audience.

Sitting on our terrace one evening, Pierre, who is just about my age, suddenly said, "You know, I am tired of being a doctor." "That's funny," I said, "I'm tired of being a headmaster. Why don't we change jobs?" He thought well of the idea, but then I added that I didn't think it would work because, whereas he wouldn't have to know anything to be a headmaster, I was afraid I probably really ought to know *something* to be a doctor. Pierre thought for a moment and then said, *"Donne-moi une heure, et je t'expliquerai tout"* ("Give me one hour, and I'll explain all you need to know"). Like all humor, that is ridiculous; but like all humor, there is just a grain of truth to it, which in this case revealed something of the quality of my friend. I have told that story to several doctors who actually did not laugh, who just looked at me as though I were being disrespectful to their profession. Naturally, they assumed that Pierre couldn't be much of a doctor to be so flip about it. But my assumption is just exactly the opposite. Nothing is more engaging than a man who does not take himself or his position too seriously.

Friendship is a mystery. What is it based upon? One generally assumes that it grows out of experiences and attitudes and interests in common and flowers through a desire to share such things. But whence comes that desire? Sue and I know hundreds of people with whom we have more in common than with these six French friends, but with only a few is the desire to share what we have as strong. There is no logic, for example, in my desire to be in Pierre's company, a man whom I had never met until I was fifty years old. Having been born and brought up in the town of Cavaillon in the Vaucluse, having studied medicine in Marseilles, having had his home occupied by German officers during the war, having served time himself as a prisoner of war, Pierre has in many ways as little in common with me in terms of what people call background as Jean, the stonemason. Yet, at a party one evening someone asked Pierre how long he had known me. Quite seriously, and without a moment's hesitation, he replied, "I've known him all my life."

One does not have to go to a second country in order to learn that there is nothing logical and a lot that is inexplicable about friendship, but for us the experience has lent a special texture to the mystery. In any case, one reason we love our second country so much is that André and Simone, Jean and Germaine, and Pierre and Micheline—as well as a host of other people—are part of our lives there. "*Et puis, voilà,*" as any one of them might say.

But America is our first country. I love America. I do not understand expatriates. When people ask me if we are going to live in France year-round after I retire,

I always say of course not. America is my home. That
is where my children live. I still have more friends there
than in France. The mission of my life is in the United
States. When we are in France, I dream a lot at night,
and I lie awake a lot, thinking. I dream and I think
about home, about my job, about the meaning of my
life, about death, mine and that of others close to me.
In the course of the summer I normally write several
hundred letters, and we run for the mail every morning.
(Communicating by the written word instead of always
by telephone is almost reason enough in itself for a
second country.) We are often homesick. We like our
American identity, and although we love to speak
French, English is our mother tongue. Each time we
leave France, we are sad. As we drive through the back
country on our way to the autoroute that leads to the
airport, I say sad, silent good-byes to the mountains
and the fields and the magpies and the *cigales* and the
wine cooperatives and the villages, just the way I did
as a small child at the end of vacation. But once on the
plane, I begin to be excited at the thought of going
home, of seeing our children and our other friends, of
becoming reinvolved in my profession, of saying precisely what I mean in my native language, of rediscov-
ering my other self. France, for us, is a second country,
but America is home.

Our second country has changed the lives of everyone
in our family. It has done a lot for us, to keep us alive,
and sane, and loving, and together.

Not-for-Profit

O NE reason America is home for me is my involvement with and commitment to what is sometimes
called the nonprofit corporation. I have spent every
minute of my professional life working for such corporations, both as an employee and as a volunteer. I
think the only corporation I ever worked for that existed in order to make a profit was the Monmouth Hotel, in Spring Lake, New Jersey, where I was a life-
guard one summer, to help defray the expenses of seminary. In addition, every minute of my formal education,
from kindergarten through graduate school, was spent
in private institutions that were incorporated not-for-
profit. In this regard I could hardly be called an average American. But the average American has had far
more involvement with not-for-profit institutions than
the average Frenchman, or the average person from almost any other country in the world. Imagine an America with no private universities, no private hospitals, no
private schools, no private museums, not to mention no

Red Cross, no Salvation Army, no Boy Scouts or Girl Scouts, no Easter Seals or March of Dimes, and no Civil Liberties Union, Common Cause, or public television! We are lucky, in America, to have a third way of getting things done, in addition to enterprises for profit and the government.

The not-for-profit institutions of America are not free from sin, or ineptitude, or corruption; but they do have certain special advantages. They generally have a relative freedom from bureaucracy, some special freedoms of choice and conviction, and, above all, a clarity of purpose. By definition and by the tax laws of the land, all not-for-profit institutions were founded for the purpose of doing good. They have no corner on that aspect of human activity; the government exists for the same purpose. But the government exists to do good in general, in a thousand directions at once, whereas the not-for-profit institution exists to do some specific good, which sometimes makes it easier for the individual (whether an employee or a volunteer) to identify himself with some special cause that particularly interests him. That is one reason America is my home, even though I greatly love my second country.

In my heart I think I must be a socialist, but in my mind I am a capitalist. I think I know the evils of capitalism as well as the next person, but I also see the not-for-profit institution, which is supported by capitalism, as a kind of saving grace, and so far more important to our way of life than the numbers it encompasses would suggest. If we are to be saved within the framework of capitalism, we need this grace. We need it as a nation, and each one of us needs it in his life. To pay taxes, vote, obey the law, and earn an honest living are not enough. To go beyond, one need not necessarily align oneself with an institution. But there are some pretty

good ones, and not to be associated in any way with any
of them would seem to me to indicate a poverty of spirit.

Having spent my professional life in the world of
private schools, it is that form of the not-for-profit
institution that interests me most and that I know
most about. It is unfortunate that to some minds the
word *private* should have bad connotations (not entirely undeserved, to be sure). In England the word
public, as regards schools, is used as we use the word
private. We mean the same thing—an institution that is
privately financed and operated but run for the public
good. Sometimes, of course, the public is selected on
some rather exclusive grounds, which is a pity. But the
overall record on that score is better than it used to be.

The world of independent schools (the name most
private schools prefer) has its own special features,
but there are parallels with and similarities to all the
other forms of not-for-profit institutions. All, for example, are directed by volunteers. Most are adminis-
tered and staffed by people who have probably made
some sort of conscious or subconscious commitment to
the well-being of others, at some sacrifice of themselves.

One beauty of not-for-profit enterprises is that they
immediately and clearly, by their very nature, put the
profit motive in a special perspective. A friend of mine,
an economist, read the first draft of this chapter for me
and objected strenuously on the grounds that it is the
profit motive that makes the world go around. That it is
one of life's most powerful forces is not being here de-
nied; but the not-for-profit institution stands as a symbol that there are other ways to urge people to get
things done.

If not for profit, then for what? If one is speaking
of a hospital, for the best possible care of the sick and
the dying; of the Red Cross, for coping with human

disaster; of a school, for providing the best possible education of the young; of a church, for providing a place conducive to worship and a leadership for pastoral care. That is what the institution is *for*.

What it is *not* for is profit. Does that mean that there *can't* be a profit? Almost invariably, yes. If there is profit, probably something is wrong. In the early days of private schools in America, there were quite a few that were proprietary—most of the military schools and many of the girls' schools. In my opinion, not one of them, *not one*, was a great educational institution, at least not until after they had incorporated not-for-profit. And even then, many of them continued to show signs of a weakness caused by a hampered early vision. Where there is a profit in a school, probably the students are not being fed as well as they should be, or there are not enough scholarships being given, or the faculty is underpaid. If the institution is not-for-profit, there *ought not* to be any profit.

The Reverend Donald B. Aldrich was rector of the Church of the Ascension in New York City for twenty years. During his tenure the church was full every Sunday, and now, more than thirty years later, I still keep running into people whose lives he touched and helped as a pastor. One day, a year after he had left the Ascension, he had lunch with the treasurer, who said, "Donald, things are going wonderfully well at the church. Do you know that for the first time in twenty years we have a balanced budget? Isn't that wonderful?" Dr. Aldrich just looked at him and said, "What would you think if I took twenty thousand one-dollar bills and went to the window and threw them out? That is what you have just done. The church does not exist to balance its budget. I always made it a point never to have a balanced budget. That way some people gave more, which was good for them, and the church was able to do more for others, which was good for them."

Of course there is such a thing as fiscal responsibility, and it is inevitable that boards of not-for-profit organizations should spend a great deal of time with budgets. Budgets can be very interesting things. They demonstrate priorities. Jesus said, "Where your treasure is, there will your heart be also." Putting a little English on that, one might say that where your heart is, there will your treasure be also. Schools that give away only 1 or 2 percent of their income on scholarships simply do not believe in scholarships, no matter what their catalogs may say. The late Alfred Howell, for many years a trustee of Wooster, used to say at almost every meeting, like the Delphic Oracle, "You've got to make the words fit the music!" True! True! And worth repeating at every meeting of the board. But also worth repeating at every meeting is the question "What's the name of the tune?"

Survival of the institution is important. That's what Alfred Howell was talking about; and that's the penultimate responsibility of boards. The ultimate responsibility is to be true to the mission for which the institution was founded. I have heard more than one petty, penny-pinching businessman—not all businessmen, or even most; just petty, penny-pinching ones— decry deficits with the words "Why can't this school be run like any other business, on a business basis?" The answer is simple. It's not a business! There are *no numbers* on the bottom line, only names . . . of people . . . to serve and be served.

Most not-for-profit institutions started as dreams, as visions, or as spontaneous inspirations. They started with a burning zeal on the part of some one person or small group to do something good. In this sense, and often in a more literal and orthodox sense, they all have a religious base. Then, in the course of time, little by little, the dreams, visions, ideals, inspirations, and zeal become institutionalized—in order that they may survive.

The process has always fascinated me, because it is inevitable and necessary, and because it never quite works, usually resulting in the destruction or at least the vitiation of the original idea. At the same time, if it is not institutionalized, it is almost sure to die. When John Coburn said "What the hell" to my fears that under my neophyte leadership the institution his father had created might perish, it gave me great courage. My interest from the beginning was pastoral, and for that I thought I already had a few qualifications and a clear commitment. But the preserving and building of an institution through which my colleagues and I could operate was something to which I had never given a moment's thought, that I knew I knew nothing about, and that, initially at least, I found relatively boring. John was assuring me, I thought, that the mission came first and the institution second.

Throughout my professional life I have continued to see things that way, but in the course of time I got caught, like everyone else. We needed a new building. We needed a stronger board of trustees and a stronger faculty. Someone suggested that we pay off a few debts. Someone else died and left us some money for endowment. A few teachers stuck around long enough to retire and to need pensions. My father once asked me if I intended to spend my whole life at Wooster. (I had been there for about fifteen years at the time.) I replied that I didn't know, that I hadn't decided. He said, "Well, son, you might as well realize that the circumstantial evidence is building up." So it was. More

and more I found myself spending time and energy
and concern, and even passion, fighting to build and
strengthen an institution.

What happens when a dream, or a vision, or a spontaneous inspiration, gets institutionalized? On Christmas Eve, 1931, a group of young Wooster alumni and
their girl friends ended an evening on the town at the
headmaster's house at Wooster. The new chapel had
just been dedicated a month before, and on a spontaneous inspiration (or so the story has been told me)
the headmaster suggested that they all walk over to the
chapel for a midnight communion service. A tradition
was started.

When I became headmaster twelve years later I was
told that this was one of the most sacred traditions of
the school—a communion service at midnight on Christmas Eve, for the alumni. I accepted the notion skep-
tically, having a little trouble imagining anyone who
would choose to go back to his old school for such
a reason on such a night. During my first couple of
years the war was still on and the turnout was small,
mostly parents of alumni in service. But on the first
Christmas Eve after the war I was amazed. The chapel
was full. And so has it been ever since. But my efforts
to preserve the essence of this magnificent inspiration
have been only partly successful.

On Christmas Eve, 1979, I conducted this service
for the thirty-fifth time in my life. There were nearly
three hundred people present, some of them having
come as far as a hundred miles. As I looked out at the
sea of joyful faces in the soft candlelight, to the sound
of carols and the smell of pine boughs, I recognized
almost everyone. I realized that this service had indeed
become an institution—and so had Wooster School.

Whether I liked it or not, whether I had helped bring it about or not, my life had become entwined in an institution about the continued existence of which one could no longer afford to be cavalier, to say, simply, "What the hell." Indeed, having resigned as headmaster in 1976, I had begun to spend much of my time trying to raise money to keep the institution alive! No more contact with students, not much time for pastoral care. That is left to others. I had become a corporate executive, devoted to the preservation of the corporation.

And yet that Christmas Eve service in 1979 was not the same, not like the good old days (or "good old daze," as a friend of mine once put it). Many years ago my wife and I decided to add an *agape* to the *eucharist*, that is, a pagan feast after the religious celebration. Until the crowds got too big, we had it in the headmaster's house. Then we moved it to the school dining room, and the presiding officer became, instead of my wife, George Schmidt, the school chef, who has been around long enough to know several generations of alumni himself. George's spreads quickly became famous, and the suspicion was born that some people came for the feast and not for the service. In 1979 I saw something that confirmed those suspicions. Two young men arrived at the service just as it was ending, each with a cup of coffee in one hand and a doughnut in the other. (George had at least succeeded in keeping them from the best of his Christmas delicacies.) Obviously they had arrived in plenty of time for the service, but had chosen to start at the back end of the festivities.

The spontaneous inspiration of December 24, 1931, had indeed become institutionalized and thereby preserved. But something had been lost.

The Christian Church itself is a case in point. It was created as an institution to preserve for all time the teachings and the spirit of Jesus Christ. Sometimes it is called the Body of Christ, and like any body, sometimes it becomes sick and diseased. So it has been that in the name of the spirit of Jesus Christ, the Christian Church, created to preserve that spirit, has been guilty of the Crusades, the Inquisition, the Salem witch-hunts, and the settling (*unsettling* would be a better word) of South America, Florida, and California (among other places) at the expense of the lives and the ways of life of millions of previous inhabitants. In the name of Jesus Christ, the West fought with fellow Christians in the Middle East. Recently my own church, the Episcopal Church, has fought within *itself* over what words to use when it prays to its Lord and whether or not a woman can lead people in the worship of that Lord as well as a man. If the purpose of the institutional church is to preserve the spirit of Jesus Christ, there seems to be an embarrassing amount of evidence that it has not always succeeded very well. But if there had been no institution, the spirit surely would have been lost. So we're damned if we do and damned if we don't.

Happily, there is an extenuating circumstance. Institutions are composed of people. And people have a way of recapturing or re-creating or revitalizing a spirit. So the Christian church, twelve hundred years after the death of Christ, with all of its sins on its head, produced St. Francis of Assisi. And then Martin Luther, and Thomas Aquinas, and Thomas a Kempis, and Martin Luther King, Jr., and Mother Theresa, as well as millions of others, some less well known, but perhaps not less worthy.

An institution is a kind of soil. Sometimes it is too

rocky for the seeds that fall on it to grow; sometimes it is too well traveled; and sometimes there are too many weeds. But sometimes the soil has been husbanded and will allow a seed to grow into something that will adorn the landscape, or feed the hungry.

Lengthened Shadows

THIS book is dedicated to three friends who have been my colleagues for almost my entire professional life. I have chosen them out of friendship, out of deep indebtedness, but also (I suspect) as a protest against the Emersonian theory that an institution is but the lengthened shadow of one man. When someone says to me, as some have on occasion, "But, John, of course you realize that *you are* Wooster School," I am not complimented. I am not pleased. I am angry and embarrassed. I know, better than anyone else, what the school owes these three men, as well as many others; and I am insulted at the suggestion that anyone should think that I don't. What is true of Wooster is true of every school. What they are is the result of the dedication and talent of a great many people, over long periods of time.

At the same time, Ralph Waldo Emerson was a pretty smart fellow, and I guess I sort of know what he meant. I think what he said has to do with the creating or the recapturing of a spirit, something to do with breathing life into forms and structures—which leads me back to my metier, the independent school world.

In deference to Emerson, I have to admit that when one thinks of Exeter, one thinks of Lewis Perry; and when one thinks of Deerfield, one thinks of Frank Boyden; and when one thinks of Groton, one thinks of Endicott Peabody; and when one thinks of Kent, one thinks of Father Sill. I also have to admit that insofar as those schools have resisted the processes of institutionalization (which, of course, they have not altogether), it is because of the stamp that those men put upon their schools by the strength of their personalities and the years of their service. The philosopher T. M. Greene once described independent schools to a group of Connecticut headmasters as consisting of *structure* and *texture*. The structure is the institution, the thing that makes a school different from a hospital. The texture is the combination of qualities that makes one school different from another. It is the individuality of the heads that has supplied or nurtured that texture.

Every profession has its galaxy of stars, powerful personifications of ideas and ideals. The school world is no exception, and the stars in my profession have shone brightly enough to light up the sky for me. Among the headmasters I have known, there have been some great men, men who would have been great in any profession. That I should write of headmasters and not of headmistresses is not because of any personal male chauvinism. I simply never knew many of the latter very well. Our worlds were more or less separate, which *is* an indication that male chauvinism was (and is) alive and well, whatever marks I may personally be given on the subject.

Because I became a headmaster in 1943, I met many

from several generations. From two generations ahead of me I met Peabody of Groton, Sill of Kent, George St. John of Choate, and Perry of Exeter. All were old men by then, not the men they had been. But the light had not gone out, and it was my privilege to catch a glimpse of it in the eye of each. For me, it counted for something. When Endicott Peabody and I shook hands one day when he was visiting the seminary where I was studying, neither of us knew that together we would span nearly one hundred years of head-mastering.

Moving as it was for me to have met these ancient heroes, the active headmasters of that time had far more influence upon me. Some of them took a direct personal interest in my career from the outset; others simply went out of their way to be considerate and helpful. Allan Heely of Lawrenceville and George Van Santvoord of Hotchkiss immediately put me on their annual preaching schedules, as did Bill Saltonstall of Exeter not long afterwards. They did it not so much because they thought I had anything particularly persuasive to say to their students, but in order to give me a little boost, a vote of confidence. When I asked Jack Crocker, Endicott Peabody's successor as headmaster of Groton, to come to Wooster to preach to our boys, he came right away, as though he had nothing more pressing to do. When a dissatisfied Wooster parent decided to take her son out of Wooster and send him to Taft, I got a phone call from Paul Cruickshank, the headmaster. "John, a Mrs. Stanley and her son Albert are sitting outside my office. I have told them that I will not see them until I have spoken with you. What would you like me to do?" Those were the days, during the Second World War, when no school was so full that it could not have taken in one more student and when, therefore, such courtesy and consideration cost something, especially since it was extended to a small young school that most people had never heard of.

One day my wife and I were invited to have lunch with Dr. and Mrs. Frank Boyden at their home on the Deerfield campus. During lunch they told us all we would ever have to know about fund raising, as well as asked us much about ourselves and our school. Why did they bother? I didn't go to Deerfield. Our school was not a close neighbor. There was no connection!

With one such experience after another, it began to dawn on me that I had joined a profession that included a great many men of very high quality. I found myself surrounded by a remarkable group of father figures. Without their help and encouragement, I might not have been able to survive long enough to learn my trade.

In the course of time, there were brother figures as well, my contemporaries, and eventually many younger than I. They are too numerous to name, but against the loneliness of the top job we have given each other comfort through the years.

Among the headmasters I have known personally, twelve founded their own schools, involving such seemingly ancient and ageless institutions as Groton, Kent, Loomis, Millbrook, Webb (in California), Brooks, South Kent, and the Church Farm School. This last is of special interest. To most minds it is not among the nationally famous independent schools; but it ought to be. It illustrates how *independent* independent schools can be, and how dangerous it is to generalize. For instance: As of this writing, if you have more than one parent, or can afford to pay more than $1,000 in tuition, you are not eligible to attend. Its founder, the Reverend Charles Shreiner, the seminary roommate of

Aaron Coburn, is the only man in the world, so far as I know, ever to pray for me in public, by my name. He did so in the Wooster chapel the day I officially became its headmaster.

If founders were a special breed, greatly to be admired and revered, so are successors to founders a special breed—though generally less admired and revered. I was one. Seemingly, I had it easier than most because my predecessor, Aaron Coburn, had died before I arrived. But it was not so. His ghost haunted me in my dreams, night after night, for a year and a half. The scenario was always the same. He would show up, his hands in his pockets, and indicate, without a word, that he wanted me to take him on a tour of the campus. On his face was a look of neither approval or disapproval. He never spoke. After I got over my reverence and awe—and my nightmare—I sometimes wondered if indeed it wasn't easier to found a school than to succeed a founder.

During my professional life I have known probably two hundred headmasters. Some I have known only casually, some intimately, and some I count among my life's best friends. Thirty seemed to me to be stars of one sort or another, and I asked myself what qualities they have in common, what special texture of their lives has enabled them to keep their schools from becoming too institutionalized.

Obviously, they were all men of authority. Horace Taft, whom I never met, tells the story of a farmer who sent his son to an independent boarding school. Dr. Taft never said the school was his own, but it might have been. Early in the year the son got into trouble and the headmaster sent him home. The father, having paid his tuition, sent him back. The headmaster, firm in his conviction, sent him home again. The father, equally firm, *brought* his son back and demanded to see the headmaster. The latter explained the situation, after which the father, more puzzled than convinced, said, "As far as I can make out, you run this school any way you damn please." The headmaster bowed politely and said, "Sir, your language is coarse and your manner offensive, but *you have grasped the idea.*"

It was also Horace Taft who dealt with a ticklish question posed by his nephew, the future Senator Robert Taft. The school had a hard-and-fast rule against weekends away for any purpose whatever. Robert wanted a weekend so that he could attend the inauguration, as president of the United States, of his father, William Howard Taft. He went to his headmaster uncle to plead. Horace Taft said he'd give his decision in the morning. True to his word, he got up in assembly the following morning and announced, "Boys, there has been a change made in the weekend rules for Taft School. From now on, any boy whose father is elected president of the United States may have a weekend to attend the inauguration."

Speaking of inaugurations, the most lavish I ever attended was that of John Kemper of Andover. It was almost presidential. There were academic processions, and fine feasts, stirring music, and many wonderful speeches by famous people. It lasted all day, a classically beautiful New England fall day. When it was over, I drove to Exeter with my friend Wells Kerr, who had been my companion throughout the festivities. Wells, who never criticized anyone directly but who was a master of the subtle hint, said, "Wasn't that a wonderful day! Just grand! Everything was perfect. . . . Of course, I couldn't help thinking of Lewis Perry's inauguration at Exeter. On his first day he simply entered chapel in the morning with the chaplain, who turned to the students and said, 'Boys, stand up. . . . Boys, meet the new principal. . . . Boys, sit down.' " William Saltonstall authenticates the story in his book *Lewis Perry of Exeter*. But fanfare or no, Lewis Perry and John Kemper were both men of authority.

Great headmasters have come in all shapes and sizes and ages, and as well as being authority figures, they have been individualists. The stereotype—smoking a pipe, with leather patches on the elbows of his sports jacket—is a myth. Claude Allen, retired headmaster of Hebron Academy, tells the story of visiting a famous boys' camp one summer with Frank Boyden. Word spread quickly through the camp that the great man was on tour. Claude, six feet two, led the way, followed by Dr. Boyden, five feet two, trying to keep up. Whispers accompanied them on their way. "So that's the great Frank Boyden! Wow! . . . But who's that little guy bringing up the rear?"

Allan Heely (some called him the Smooth Moose) would have been at home with Queen Elizabeth I or II. George Van Santvoord could have been mistaken for a member of the Institute for Advanced Study. Frank Boyden, who spent his spring vacations visiting various major-league baseball camps in Florida, probably actually did delight in the company of Joe Cronin and Ted Williams of Boston Red Sox fame. Arthur ("Monk") Terry, of Middlesex, could substitute any time for Bob Hope. And Howard Jones, of Northfield–Mount Hermon, could just as easily have been a senior officer with Merrill Lynch. There you have it. What kind of man makes a great headmaster? A courtier? An intellectual? A baseball fan? A stand-up comedian? A stockbroker?

Different in style, they were alike in morality.

Thomas Carlyle's ideal government, the benevolent dictatorship, has actually existed in some independent schools under the leadership of some great headmasters. But benevolence should not be confused with sweet sentimentality. Almost always there has been too little money, thus presenting headmasters with hard choices —often between the students (the paying customers and the product) and the faculty (the life blood and the means of production). Because most teachers choose their profession, and more or less consciously choose a lifetime of relative poverty at the same time, they are often easy to take advantage of. Sometimes nothing stands between them and hardship or suffering but the morality of the head. Over nearly forty years, I have watched the lot of the teacher in a great many schools steadily improve, not because of unions or collective bargaining, but because of the caring of the man at the top.

A one-time member of the Wooster faculty, Richard Jackson, was crippled by polio at a very early age. Then as a fairly young man he became very deaf. Despite these handicaps, he enjoyed thirty years as an outstanding history teacher, greatly loved and respected by his students and by his colleagues. But at sixty-two, when I first met him, he was like a man twenty years older. Wanting to strengthen the faculty quickly, I was tempted to let him go on the grounds that he could be replaced by a better teacher. As he had been at Wooster only five years, I could have done so with a relatively clear conscience. But my colleagues persuaded me that the lesson to be taught of how a handicapped, older man should be treated was more important than the teaching of history, which was adequate. He stayed on for five more years.

The caring extends beyond the faculty. A friend of

mine, the son of a missionary, arrived alone in this
country to attend Hotchkiss, only to find that there
was no room and no scholarship money available.
George Van Santvoord not only found him a place in
another school, but personally paid part of his tuition
—for four years!

Almost the first thing I did when I became a headmaster was to call my old headmaster, Charles H.
Breed, of Blair Academy, to ask his advice. Without a
moment's hesitation he said. "Lock your goat in the
closet and don't let anyone get it." When he finally
retired, his wife told me that he had reached that decision because he woke up once in the middle of the night
and there was his goat, out of the closet, walking around
the bed. I learned early that the best weapon for keeping people from getting your goat is laughter. In *The
Thirteen Clocks*, James Thurber tells a fairy tale about
a handsome young prince who tries to win the heart and
hand of a beautiful young princess, struggling against
the constant interference of a wicked witch. He is
helped in his efforts by a good spirit whose name is
Golog. In the end, the prince wins the princess and
rides off with her into the sunset on his magnificent
white horse. As they disappear over the horizon, Golog
waves to them and says, "Remember laughter. You'll
need it, even in the blessed isles of Ever After."

Of all the qualities that great headmasters have in
common, the most important and the most obvious is
the capacity for laughter. It is a good thing because
they need it, not only in "the blessed isles of Ever
After," but in the often unblessed isles of Here and
Now. In fact, it could almost be said that any headmaster without a generous capacity for laughter just
can't be a great headmaster.

In 1954 I was elected to a rather quaint organization known as the Headmasters Association, sometimes referred to by its members simply as "*the* Headmasters." It meets for three days each year, and its purposes seem to be twofold: to argue endlessly as to what its purpose is—and to laugh, at each other and with each other. The funniest speech I ever heard in my life was one delivered my first year by Thompson Webb, the founder of the Webb School in Claremont, California, and the son of the founder of the Webb School in Bell Buckle, Tennessee. All he did was tell the story of the founding of his school, but it was a study of self-ridicule worthy of Jack Benny.

Members come to the meetings armed with pens and notebooks, not to record gems of educational wisdom, but to record each other's jokes and anecdotes. If the notebooks are not full at the end of the three days, the meeting has not been a good one. Arthur Perry, of Milton Academy, caught the essence with the story of a man who frequented a particular bordello. He and the madam became good friends, and he was surprised one day to find her lined up with the girls. To his request for an explanation she replied, "Oh, I don't know. Some days it just seems as though I can't *stand* any more administration!"

Because not-for-profit institutions exist to do good, their mission is deadly serious, particularly since the failure to do good usually means doing harm. But there is a difference between taking the mission seriously and taking oneself seriously. The latter can be fatal. One day a very bright, self-important young teacher, just out of college, sporting his Phi Beta Kappa key, committed the latest in a whole series of dumb, inept, and publicly embarrassing acts that he had become famous for since the beginning of the school year. I can't remember what it was—evidence that it wasn't serious. But I know that it was totally exasperating. Contrary to popular belief, headmasters' hair turns white or falls out, not because of what students do, but because of new young teachers. They arrive knowing so much, yet with *everything* still to learn. Some become great teachers in the course of time, others become very good ones, and some leave the profession early. But almost all of them are headaches in the beginning. On this particular occasion, for some reason or other, I was more discouraged than usual and said to the dean, as he followed me into my office, "Oh, Donald, what am I going to *do?*" He said, "It's simple. Charge him tuition." As I burst out laughing, he added, "Ya gotta laugh or go crazy."

I cannot imagine that other kinds of not-for-profit institutions are very different in this regard.

Finally, tenure. Each of those great headmasters stayed in one place a long time. By a long time I mean twenty-five to fifty years! Frank Boyden, for sixty-two years the headmaster of Deerfield, probably holds the record. But Endicott Peabody was not far behind. Like Henry Aaron's home-run record, such performances require a lot of luck and good health. But they also require a certain attitude of mind and some philosophical presuppositions. One thing those great headmasters had in common was that they were seldom tempted by greener grass on the other side of fences.

Today, some of the old attitudes and presuppositions are being challenged. Some modern headmasters argue that there is such a thing as staying too long. Of course there is. But since the purported average tenure of headmasters today is four to six years, one could also argue that there is such a thing as staying too short a time. The current explanation from the lips and pens of headmasters who have resigned after three to six years is "I have accomplished what I came here to accomplish." Now, just what does that mean? Certainly not what it says.

One thing is certain. No institution that is not-for-profit has any chance of preserving its individuality for long unless someone at the top sticks with it for most of his life. That is one reason I never left Wooster. My predecessor fed me the line. When he was once offered the headmastership of another school (a very prestigious one), he said, "I've already got a school. What the hell do I want with another?" Builders of most institutions need to keep going onward and upward. But people whose major mission in life is the education of the young don't need to. They can afford just to keep going onward and onward.

No school is merely the lengthened shadow of one man. But single personalities at the head, with certain qualities of character, who are willing to give a fair chunk of the years of their lives to one place, can help keep a spirit and an ideal alive against the onslaughts of institutionalization.

A former dean of St. Paul's Cathedral, in Boston, once told me that he thought all church buildings should be prefabricated structures that could be dismantled and moved as soon as the guiding spirit of the parish was gone. "Then let the people start over with nothing and build something new from the beginning again. Or let the parish die." In some ways I find that a delightful thought. But you can't do that. An institution must be formed, and preserved, and has to take on ever more structure. One can only hope that strong individuals will come along now and then to breathe new life into it, to refurbish its special texture.

Trustees

———◆———

WHEREVER there are lengthened shadows, one will always find standing around in the shade some remarkable people, such people as one does not normally think of as standing around in anybody else's shadow, people like Cyrus Vance of Kent, the Thomas Lamonts—father and son—of Exeter, Bishop William Lawrence of Groton, Henry Luce of Hotchkiss, Bruce Barton of Deerfield. These are the trustees, the unsung heroes, the volunteers, the people whose unselfish devotion of time, talent, and means make the not-for-profit institutions of America possible. They are not all famous. They are not all wealthy. They are not all purely motivated. Some are on ego trips. Some are wealthy but not generous. Some are meddlesome. Some are downright vicious. But on the whole, they are part of a remarkable tradition. I have talked about this with many of my French friends from comparable walks of life. They have never heard of such a thing—in theory, yes, but not in degree of commitment and dedication and giving. And *noblesse oblige* is a French phrase!

Like most young people, I grew up unaware of my debt to this rather special American army. I had spent eleven years in four not-for-profit educational institutions without ever wondering who was on their boards or what they did. I was therefore unprepared and awed by the fact that a man of Dr. Allen O. Whipple's caliber and national importance would be serving as a trustee of Wooster, let alone as president of its board. In subsequent years, inspired by Dr. Whipple's example, and by way of repaying a debt to society that had accrued through the voluntary services of a good many trustees backstage in my own life, I have always tried to say yes to invitations to serve on the boards of other institutions. Through the years this has come to include ten schools, one college, two committees of the College Entrance Examination Board, the National Association of Episcopal Schools, the Connecticut Association of Independent Schools, and several organizations not connected with education. This I record, not to boast, but to provide perspective. I have, like many others, spent literally thousands of hours at board meetings, listening to wisdom and folly, and watching the machinations of group deciding. Many of those hours have not been inspiring. But the *idea* is inspiring, the idea that so many Americans are willing to give so much of themselves for nothing—except the satisfaction of doing a little good here and there.

The importance of a board to any not-for-profit institution was borne in upon me even before I attended my first meeting. When the call came to go to Wooster, I had just been ordained to the Episcopal ministry by Bishop Henry Knox Sherrill, the bishop of Massachusetts, and I felt that I could not consider the job without his advice and consent. So I went to see him at his office at 1 Joy Street, in Boston. He looked at me in his kindly way on that day in 1942 and said that he had never heard of the Wooster School and would like to know something about it before advising me. (Years later, one of his grandsons was to become a Wooster senior prefect, and another Wooster alumnus, John Coburn, was to be one of his successors as bishop of Massachusetts, occupying that same office at 1 Joy Street.)

"Have you got a copy of the school catalog?" he asked. I did, and I handed it to him. He turned immediately to the page where the trustees were listed and never looked at anything else. He ran his finger quickly down the list and said, "Well, I don't know any of these men except Horace Taft. We are on the Yale Corporation together. Wooster looks like a pretty local outfit to me, but I'll write Horace and see what he says. If you want to jump off the end of the dock, that's all right with me. I'd just like to make sure that you don't have lead weights on your feet."

Horace Taft gave Wooster his blessing, and the bishop gave me his. But I never forgot the lesson and set about correcting the Wooster trustee situation as soon as I could. Before I had had a chance to meet him and thank him, Horace Taft died, which left the Wooster board without a single member who knew anything whatever about how to run a school. It is hard to imagine the extent of my father's panic had he realized that I was not the only one who "didn't know anything"! Against this frightening prospect, I found I had two things going for me. One was Dr. Whipple, whose name Bishop Sherrill had overlooked. The other was a tradition started by the founder of allowing the headmas-

ter to pick his own trustees, a system that sounds
horrifying in this modern world but that has sometimes
produced less horrifying results than some of the modern methods. In any case, I was given the choice and
immediately selected Dr. Charles H. Breed, then still
headmaster of Blair Academy, my alma mater. His
election was followed by that of Henry Allen Moe, an
old friend of my father's and at the time the head of
the Guggenheim Foundation. Serving as he did then on
countless organizations for good works, he was loath
to take on a little school that, like Bishop Sherrill, he
had never heard of. But unlike Bishop Sherrill, he knew
Dr. Whipple very well, and after rubbing his chin for
a few minutes, he said, "Well, I guess if Allen Whipple
can find time to help your school, I can too."

How does one get important and busy people to
serve on boards of small and relatively insignificant
institutions? Henry Moe gave me a clue to part of the
answer. He liked Dr. Whipple and enjoyed his company, and serving on the Wooster board would, among
other things, provide him with regular opportunities to
see his friend. Of course a potential board member
should have some enthusiasm for the ideals and the
mission of the institution in question. He should have
something to give that it needs and that he feels like
giving. People speak these days of the three *W*'s—
work, wisdom, and wealth. But that is more neat than
enlightening. Most institutions need a great many
different things from their trustees: special knowledge,
kinds of experiences, and varieties of attitudes. People
will generally be happy to serve as long as they feel
useful. But beyond altruism is the simple matter of
enjoying oneself, of anticipating the next meeting with
pleasure. "Well, Edith," I imagined Henry Moe saying
at breakfast, "today I must go to Wooster School for

a trustee meeting. You know, I'm rather looking forward to it. I haven't seen Allen Whipple in a long time."

In building the Wooster board, I set about trying to find busy and important people of varied experience who not only would have something to give, but who would enjoy each other's company in the process. When Dr. Whipple finally retired and became Wooster's first trustee emeritus, a board citation read, in part: "In the early days when Wooster was uncertain, unknown, and unhonored, he lent to it his name, which even then was certain, known, and honored."

What I wanted above all at the outset were men who were concerned for the goals of our school. Women didn't even occur to me until years later! Nor did wealth seem important to me right away, perhaps because, at that point, wealth was not what we needed most—and I wonder now if it ever is. Little by little an impressive team developed; deans, bishops, other headmasters, lawyers, chairmen of boards of national corporations, a museum director, a music conservatory chairman, a movie producer, bankers, another famous surgeon, two former Wooster faculty members, two foundation heads, a hospital executive, and others with special talents and concerns. Eventually there were women and, of course, some generous people of wealth.

It was not a representative board in terms of constituencies. I once served on a board that was perfect in that respect, and thus very modern. It was one of the weakest boards I was ever associated with. It had current faculty members, alumni (even though the school was so young that the oldest alumnus was still in college), current parents and past parents, a representative from the local village, and even some students. It was beautifully balanced, but there was no strength. I am not opposed to that sort of representation, and my friends tell me that these days you can't avoid it; but I believe that if a given constituency has no one available of sufficient caliber to be a good trustee —*the best that can be found*—I'd rather see it go unrepresented on the board.

For years the Wooster board was made up almost entirely of past parents. We had an unwritten rule against current parents. The explanation is written on a plaque outside the chapel door, which lists all the trustees who have ever served. There the board's function is described: "To see to it that the present is always faithful to the past, and to the future." Neither current parents, nor faculty members, nor students are generally well qualified emotionally to carry out that function. Of course there are always exceptions, some of whom have found their way onto the Wooster board. Times change and the Wooster board has changed. There are now some official representatives of various constituencies. But the best way to get the best possible board for any institution is to find the best-qualified people, even if they all come from the same constituency.

The primary responsibility of any board is to choose a head. It is not an operation that is supposed to happen very often, but when it does it tests the caliber of a board as nothing else. I have helped to do this for several schools and have seen a good many otherwise able people fall into one or another of the pitfalls involved in the process. I have fallen into more than one myself, even though I knew they were there. Nevertheless, knowing what they are helps a little.

The first is to believe that what you are looking for, and therefore are determined to find, is Sir Lancelot and Lady Guinevere. I have read at least a hundred job descriptions put out by schools on the search, and they all read the same: not even Sir Lancelot, but the Second Coming of Christ. When I once asked Wells Kerr what he thought the most important single qualification for a headmaster was, he replied instantly, "The title. If you have the title, then you're a headmaster." Another friend put it differently. "If it says 'Headmaster' on your T-shirt, then you're it." And that was the same man who once predicted that I would become "a son of a bitch, just like all the rest of them," which, presumably, Sir Lancelot would not. There is nothing wrong with dreaming, but what one is going to end up with—with luck—is a more or less normal human being, with some weaknesses and some strengths.

The second pitfall is to think that you are going to find this paragon among the unemployed, or at least among the dissatisfied; that all you have to do is let enough people know of the vacancy and wait for the applications to pour in for you to assess. This might be called the volunteer system. The English have always used it. They advertise and candidates apply. No one who does not apply is a candidate. I have always favored what might be called the draft, which involves considering people who have not applied, who might not want the job, and who might turn it down if it were offered them. The draft has some obvious difficulties and disadvantages and is more and more out of vogue these days, but it has the happy advantage of introducing people who are not unemployed and not unhappy—two rather strong initial recommendations, it seems to me.

A third pitfall is to underestimate the size of the task. In theory, we all know it is a big job that will take a lot of time, but in practice it is *always* more than we bargained for. Battle fatigue is an enemy of a good final selection. Since everyone involved is a volunteer, it is easy to argue, after a few months, that one has simply taken all the time he can afford from his own affairs.

When we were very young, most of us believed in the one-and-only theory regarding a mate for life. Then, on "some enchanted evening . . . across a crowded room" there she was! A spark in the heart gave a light to the eye and we *knew* the search was over. We might have had in mind a beautiful blond, three inches shorter than ourselves, two years younger, with a similar educational background to our own, a good tennis player, a great cook, and from a fine family. Suddenly all that goes out the window. *This is the one,* though she is nothing like what we had in mind. It is a kind of double pitfall for search committees to think (a) that this approach is irrelevant, and (b) that it is the key to the whole process. There is not a one and only candidate, and yet enchantment is to be trusted . . . within limits.

I have strong feelings about the issue of skills, training, and experience versus a kind of person. Wells Kerr used to say, "Once a headmaster, always a headmaster." Boards of trustees tend to be so impressed by experience that Wells was very nearly right. If you have ever been a headmaster, you have a good chance, an inside chance, of getting another job as a headmaster, no matter if you were good at it or not. But none of the stars whom I extolled earlier had ever been a headmaster before taking on the job that made him famous. None was ever described primarily as "an administrator." None, I suspect, would have liked to have been known as an "educator."

Frank Boyden was twenty-four years old when he became headmaster of Deerfield, with no previous

school experience. Sam Bartlett, the founder of South
Kent, started at about the same age, having taught, I
think, one year at Kent. Wooster's founder, Aaron
Coburn, had been rector of the local church and had
never taught a day in his life or even attended an independent school. Endicott Peabody had been a missionary in Arizona. John Kemper, of Andover, was a West
Point graduate and a career army officer. Ogden Miller,
of the Gunnery, had been athletic director at Yale.
What they had in common was a quality of life, not
skills, training, or experience.

The final, and most dangerous, pitfall in the process
of choosing a head is to think that the wedding is the
goal when, in fact, it is the marriage. No new head
turns out to be any more perfect than any new bride
or groom. Making the marriage work takes effort on
everyone's part, with no rest for the weary. And weary
is what search committees and boards are after the
wedding. Having resisted the temptation to quit before
the search was properly completed, now the temptation is to say, "There, we did it! We've got a *great*
person. Now I can go back to the regular business of
my life and let him or her run the school."

Earlier I have said that one reason for the modern
fast turnover of heads of schools is the fickleness of the
heads themselves. But another is the naïveté and im-
patience of trustees. Suddenly they discover what they
should have known all along: that their chosen head
has some shortcomings after all. "Very well, we were
wrong. Let's try again." A lot of marriages that could
have been made to work break up that way, and so do
schools and heads. There are situations where fast action is called for, but they are exceptions. Most of the
time, what is required is that each side take a little
blame and give a little ground.

Trustees make decisions, and although choosing a head—or concluding that a new head is needed—is the most important decision that boards ever have to make, it is not the only one. At every meeting there are decisions—about how money shall be gathered and spent, about how people shall be treated, and about what new directions, if any, the institution shall take—decisions, in other words, that will ensure that "the present is always faithful to the past and to the future."

The process of group decision making is different from that of individual decision making in that the responsibility is shared, and thus the agony and loneliness are softened. Members of groups reaching a group conclusion can lean on each other, even hide behind each other. It is a kind of semifinal as compared with a final choice. First each person makes up his own mind, knowing all the time that what he decides may or may not be what is finally decided. The final decision is reached by a lot of people raising their hands and someone counting votes. It is not the same process, for example, as that by which General Eisenhower decided, in 1942, that D-Day would be June 6. In *The Longest Day*, Cornelius Ryan has painted a striking picture of how that came about. The general is surrounded by his chief advisers, each an expert in his field and each with his own idea as to when the invasion should take place, and why. The general goes around the room, asking each man for his opinion and his reasons. Then there is silence . . . two minutes . . . five minutes . . . an eternity . . . while the final decision is made in the mind of one man. Finally, Eisenhower speaks. "D-Day will be June 6."

There is no way that boards of trustees can avoid the relative tentativeness of voting as compared with one person's deciding. The best an individual member

can do is to keep reminding himself that it behooves
him always to vote *as though* the decision were his to
make—with all the attendant loneliness and agony. It
is a special weakness of those of us who have served on
boards that we don't do this often enough or carefully
enough. So it is that board decisions are too often seen
by others as irresponsible.

The board of a reputable girls' school appointed as
its head a woman of some considerable years of experience at another school, uprooting her from a job and
a community where she had spent most of her life. Half-
way through her second year, a special board meeting
was called in which it was affirmed that the faculty, the
students, and the parents were up in arms, that the
head had totally lost their confidence, and that she had
been persuaded to submit her resignation. The meeting
had been called to act upon it. Two men squared off
against each other, one for accepting the resignation
and the other opposed on the grounds that the decision was immorally precipitous and that the board had
not even tried to be supportive of her position.

After heated debate, the vote was cast 17–4 in favor
of accepting her resignation. The president then said,
"I think it is terribly important that we present a
united front to our public, and I hope therefore that
we can make this vote unanimous." The leader of the
opposition objected strenuously. "How can we pretend
to be united when we are not? I propose that every
member of this board put his or her membership on
the line with his or her vote. That's what I intend to do.
The day the headmistress leaves the campus, I will
resign. I hope the others who voted with me will do the
same. That way the board will be united, and we won't
be kidding anyone." His leading opponent jumped to
his feet and said, "I agree." So it was until a week later,

when another emergency meeting was called. It seems that all hell had broken loose. The original information proved to have been false, and the faculty and parents and students in droves came to the defense of their headmistress. The game of the week before was re-played, with the same pitchers and line-up. Only this time, the vote was exactly 17–4 the other way. The original dissident repeated his speech about putting one's membership on the line with his vote, and his opponent had no choice but to agree. The sad lesson is that through all the deliberations, only eight people really knew what they thought, whereas thirteen hid behind the convictions of others.

Another case in point: A particular board was discussing the possibility of cutting its scholarship allotment as a way of balancing the budget. Of course it would mean a decrease in the number of underprivileged students who could be accepted, but, as one very articulate, persuasive member put it, "It seems to me that we have clearly demonstrated that our school is not exclusive. All you have to do is consider so-and-so and so-and-so, and anyone from the outside can see that we accept all kinds of students from all walks of life." "Hear! Hear!" echoed around the room like a shot, and a vote was just about to be taken that would have been overwhelming when someone else spoke up. "Nonsense! That issue is never clear. No private school ever does enough in this regard. And no matter how much it does, of course it is exclusive. The world is watching—the public world, the taxpaying world, the excluded world. Cutting scholarships is absolutely the last thing this institution should do at this time." The tide changed, and the vote was overwhelming, only the other way. I was in the room at the time, and what interested me most was not the outcome of the vote, but how easily and quickly twenty good, intelligent, well-meaning people had changed their minds.

The fight for survival is, of course, a major and constant preoccupation of most boards. It is the hidden agenda of all but a handful of the strongest institutions. For two years I served on the board of Bennett College, the last two years of its existence. The reasons I served were that the president was a close personal friend, I knew they were in trouble, and I thought I might be able to help. Secretly, I suppose, I was also curious to see how a not-for-profit corporation would go out of business, if that was to be its fate. As it turned out, I was of no help, but I learned a great deal.

"Ladies and gentlemen, we are all that is left of Bennett College." With these words the president opened a meeting held in a member's windowless New York City office, far from the beautiful campus in Millbrook, New York. "There are no undergraduates," he went on. "There is no faculty. We have no employees. The buildings and land are no longer ours. Our remaining responsibilities are to creditors, to the State of New York, which issued our original charter, and to all living graduates of the college."

In spite of the fact that we had all been prepared by countless meetings and constant reports, a shocked silence met the actuality of those words. My first thought, once I started thinking again, was that every member of every board of every not-for-profit organization in America should sit in such a room and hear such words just once. Once is enough. Crystallized in that room that morning was the ultimate responsibility of a board of trustees, whether it is of a school or a museum or a hospital or a church or a Boy Scout troop or the Red Cross or the Legal Aid Society. While the institution is flourishing, it is the board's responsibility to see that people are treated right, that the mission for which the institution was created is adhered to, and that all decisions are fiscally sound. But when the institution ceases to function, for whatever reason, the board's responsibility is to take the rap and to see that all procedures in connection with its closing are moral.

The Bennett board that I joined was an exceptionally good one, led by a superb president. It was devoted, incredibly generous in a losing cause, and thoroughly ethical and sensitive in all of its deliberations to the last day. The crisis brought out the very best in everyone. The trouble was, I suspect, that the crisis was not perceived as a crisis until it was too late. Too many decisions had been made with too little thought for too long, and recovery finally was not possible. There, but for the grace of God, goes any institution run by any board.

An ideal board member for any not-for-profit organization? My model would be the late R. Lee Waterman, for twenty-five years a trustee of Wooster School and for seventeen of those years president of the board. If Wooster School has any strength as an institution and any fidelity to its mission, it is largely because for more than half of its first fifty years, its board was under the leadership of Allen Whipple and Lee Waterman. Mr. Waterman's connection with Wooster began when his son became a student there. At that time he was vice-president of the Alexander Smith Carpet Company, and he and his family lived in Wilton, Connecticut, not far from the school. He was such an impressive person to meet and talk to that he was soon asked if he would join the Wooster board, thereby breaking the rule of no current parents. It was not long, however, before he was given an opportunity to show that he was the perfect exception for proving the rule. His son, George, began to chafe early under the Wooster regime, and it became increasingly clear to everyone (including George) that he and the school were not for each other. George's version today is that I kicked him out. My version is that I told him that if things really got too much for him, all he had to do was tell me, that he didn't really have to force the issue by doing something to get kicked out. That we are friends today is evidence that the question of whether he jumped or was pushed isn't very important. The star of the show was George's father, who managed the rare balancing act of being a supportive father and a good trustee at the same time. It was on the strength of that performance that I asked him if he would consider being board president. In retrospect, I am quite certain that the texture of Lee Waterman's performance as a trustee and a board president, through many ensuing years, was determined by that early incident.

The vice-presidency of Alexander Smith was not a position in the world of commerce and industry of any great glamour or prestige, but it was more so than being unemployed; and it was not long after Lee became our president that he resigned from his position and was, indeed, unemployed—for better than two years. He was not worried, and neither was I; so little, in fact, that we made a joke about it, and I was sorely tempted to so list our president in the school catalog. He amused himself, incidentally, during those two years by becoming a consultant to the *Reader's Digest* when that magazine first decided to take on advertising. Then, when we learned that he had accepted a position as vice-president of the Corning Glass Works, and that he and his family would be moving to Corning, New York, I was sure that we had lost our man. But he continued to serve our board as faithfully as ever, even after he became Corning's president.

Lee was a graduate of a public high school and had no contact with any independent school, so far as I know, except the one from which his son had been "kicked out." He was also a graduate of Bates College, as a science major, and he served on the Bates board for almost as many years as he did on the Wooster board. I believe that during the nearly thirty years that I knew him those were the only two not-for-profit boards he served on, not counting boards of local organizations. For the ideal trustee, that is important since, ideally, one should not spread oneself too thin. Lee was able to give the impression, as Dr. Whipple had before him, that he had nothing on his mind or on his schedule more important than the affairs of Wooster School. I am sure he gave Bates the same impression. When he died, he left the bulk of his modest estate, after family considerations, to those two institutions—equally.

Abraham Lincoln once said that after the age of forty, a man should be held responsible for everything about himself, including his physical appearance, implying that most of us grow to look like what we are. Lee Waterman was physically an impressive man, standing about six feet three, with a frame that exuded strength. He had had polio as a boy and walked with a slight limp, but even that weakness exuded strength. Once, when he was in his late fifties, he broke his good leg and was in a wheelchair for several months. Even in the wheelchair he exuded strength. His eyes were bright, bright blue and were always moving and sparkling. But there was nothing furtive about the movement; he was simply looking at everything, and *seeing everything.* He saw tiny fishing boats way across Lake

Kiuka, from the porch of his lakeside cottage; he saw the movement of clouds in the distance while cruising in the Caribbean; he saw the top of Mont Ventoux from our terrace in southern France; he saw expressions of discontent in the faces of Wooster students in the late sixties; he saw trouble coming, and hope beyond. He saw problems and solutions in the same glance. Paraphrasing words from the Gospel of St. Mark, he had eyes and he saw; he had ears and he heard; and he understood.

He had very big hands, the fingers on one having been slightly deformed by some sort of accident. During board meetings he would sit back and listen to others (he was good at that), never wanting anyone to leave a meeting frustrated by the feeling that he had not had a chance to say his piece. Then, just at the right moment, he would lift up his hands, palms out and fingers spread wide, and quietly pull everything together. There is a prayer that I have used many times that includes the words "Grant calmness and control of thought." A thousand times the Lord has granted just that to Wooster board meetings through the person of his servant, Lee Waterman.

When a problem was presented, he would *immediately* grasp the moral implications, and by grasp I mean *"reach out and take hold of and hang onto."* Since all not-for-profit organizations exist above all for moral purposes, that is an essential quality in an ideal trustee.

He saw the institution simply as a collection of people, which in itself takes no great wisdom. But he saw his job as a trustee as being first and foremost to be concerned with the well-being of those people, trusting that if he did his job, they would do theirs of running the institution day by day. That concern started with the head man, myself, and my family. Every year he took the initiative with regard to my salary and my living conditions. I never asked for a raise in my life; indeed, sometimes I objected on the grounds that my salary was too much in comparison with the salaries of my colleagues on the faculty and staff. "The answer to that," he said, "is not to keep your salary closer to theirs, but for you to fight to get theirs closer to yours. As long as you are willing to be underpaid, they will have no champion to see that they are not." Once, when I was in France for a year's sabbatical, he wrote me a letter out of the blue and said, "I think it is time we did something about the headmaster's house. You have lived in it, more or less as it was when you moved in, for twenty years, during which time your family has grown and the school has grown. Talk to Suzanne and tell me what you think you need most." The answer was a new kitchen. The kitchen we got was so magnificent that it was featured in *House Beautiful* and in an article by Craig Claiborne in the *New York Times*.

Periodically he would call me between meetings, just to find out how I was and how things were going at the school. Twice he called during the sometimes dreary months of winter and said, "Virginia and I have chartered a small yacht that sleeps four plus the crew, and we plan to cruise the British Virgin Islands for a week. I think it would be a good thing for the school if the headmaster and his wife were to take a break about now. Pack your bags and we'll meet you at the airport."

This concern for the well-being of people did not stop with the headmaster and his family. Most of the years he served, he knew most of the faculty by name and family. It was he who was largely instrumental in establishing our pension plan and in having the school buy life insurance for all employees (he knew the maintenance staff and kitchen staff as well as the faculty).

And it was he who decided that in the face of inflation, the school's contribution to the pension plan was too small and saw that something was done about it. During the time of student unrest, which was long after his own son had left school, when the word *establishment* was in ill repute, he volunteered to come down from Corning and talk to the students about what he thought that word meant, which he did with most salutary results. He loved to hear the students sing in chapel (he was, among so many other things, an amateur musician), but he was not sentimental about the younger generation; he was sensitive to their needs and their frustrations, as well as to their promise.

As has been said here and elsewhere many times, any trustee of any not-for-profit organization should be prepared to offer work or wisdom or wealth. Lee Waterman offered all three. Of his work and wisdom enough has been said. Of wealth, Lee Waterman did not have a great deal, as such things are measured in the not-for-profit world. He started slowly, though always regularly. As he could, he gave. Generosity is measured, according to one theory, not by how much you give, but by how much you hold back. By that measure Lee Waterman was among the most generous of men. When a new science building finally became the school's most pressing need, he gave the bulk of it—his first really big gift in terms of dollars. I wanted to name the building after him, but he objected. "No, Wooster doesn't do things that way. I think the building should be named after the most famous scientist ever connected with Wooster. That would be Dr. Whipple, wouldn't it?" At this writing, one of Wooster's finest physical facilities is the Allen O. Whipple Science Center, named after a man whom Lee Waterman had never met. I have mentioned his remembrance of Wooster in his will. He also took out a $50,000 life insurance policy on his own life with the school as beneficiary—and never told anyone about it. He gave quietly, modestly, and imaginatively. After he joined the Corning Glass Works, he arranged to have the school's dishware donated, replenishing the supply year after year for the rest of his life. Corning still continues the tradition in his honor.

He had the perspective so essential to trustees. One of his favorite phrases was *over time.* Over time . . . this or that would prove important.

Finally, he did his homework—always. He read every word of everything that was ever sent out from the school. He was always prepared for every meeting. He died a few days after a trustees meeting in April 1978. I called on him in the hospital the night before the meeting. He had almost lost the power of speech and couldn't sit up in bed, but he had read all the documents and had some helpful suggestions about certain specific items on the agenda.

Lee Waterman was the ideal trustee. Wooster has had other great trustees, and so have all good and strong not-for-profit corporations had great trustees. They wouldn't be great, couldn't be great, without them. Lee Waterman was not unique, but he was unusual.

Fathers of Sons

A SEEMING advantage of spending one's life on a school campus is that one is provided with hundreds of examples of fatherhood to choose from, some good and some indifferent and some sinfully bad. Because I was a headmaster for some years before I became a father, and for many years before I had a son the age of my students, I had a lot of time to learn. I spent that time, of course, telling others how it should be done, each year gaining more and more confidence so that I finally arrived at a point where I thought I knew all about it. It was on the nineteenth of July, 1962, my oldest son's thirteenth birthday, that I found out I was wrong.

The day started out pretty much like any other day of that summer's vacation on Cape Cod. In spite of the awesomeness of the occasion, I felt confident. I had been telling fathers for so long how to avoid the problems and the pitfalls! I had refereed a thousand father-son battles, usually siding with the son because I was sure that the son was usually right. How fortunate for my son to have such a wise and experienced father as he ventured into the unknown, sometimes frightening, sometimes exciting, sometimes boring territory of adolescence!

Then we had a fight . . . on his thirteenth birthday! Of course, I can't possibly remember what it was about (although at thirty *he* remembered). I do remember that it was both physical and verbal. I had always been a spanking father, but I had a theory that the only time spanking was justified was in anger. There was anger. And throughout the battle I could hear the voice of the wise and experienced mentor of teen-age boys in the back of my mind; "Don't spank him, you fool! He's too big for that. He's almost a man. Today! . . . And don't *say* that. That's exactly the thing *not* to say!"

And down came the hand and out came the words!

"The good that I would, I do not; and the evil that I would not, *that* I do," wrote St. Paul, who wasn't even a father.

Of course my son and I made up before he went to bed, with much embracing and tears and promises. There would still be battles, differences, separations, chasms created and then bridged over. But that night we did reach a turning point. There never was another spanking, and there was a new kind of relationship between us.

Nevertheless, I went to bed that night ashamed, and as I lay awake, a new light began to dawn. Fatherhood, I was at long last beginning to realize, is an emotional state, which all the secondhand experience in the world cannot instruct—if the moment is wrong. Eighteen

years of being a headmaster for teen-age boys and
their fathers had not taught me *one single thing* about
being a father myself.

Fatherhood is a paradox. It runs the gamut from
the glory of God to the crassness of a mere bull. The
words *God* and *father* go together because for a long
time men, in their desperate attempts to describe God,
have hit upon the analogy of a father. God is the Creator. And he is omniscient, omnipotent, and omni-
present, as well as all-loving and all-caring. He also
holds himself responsible, within certain ground rules,
for the well-being of what he has created. Of course, we
know that no father is all these things, but many people
(including fathers) think that the ideal father would
be all these things. And so we say this is what God must
be like. He is like a perfect father. Perhaps some people
believe in God just because they feel the need, more
than any other need, for such an ideal father.

Obviously there's a trap here. If we describe God as
a father, we are making certain assumptions about
what we think a father ought to be like. He ought to
be sort of like God! We then go on to bolster this extreme position. In trying our best to honor the first
president of the United States, we call him the father
of our country. If an only son dies without progeny, we
say that's the end of the line, no matter what his sisters
may have produced. After all, it's the father's name
that counts. If today there is a healthy reaction to this
sort of thinking, one must admit that it is late in coming and a long way from winning the day. When a
liberated woman keeps her maiden name after marriage
instead of taking her husband's, she is merely choosing
in favor of her father instead of her husband's father.
The idea of fatherhood is still entrenched in our society.
Fatherliness is close to godliness.

On the other hand . . . Down on the farm bulls
service cows, which is a kind of fatherhood. Among
us humans, there are fathers whose position in the family, and in society, is not any more glorious than
that. Any half-witted fourteen-year-old boy can take
a roll in the hay with his girl friend (or anyone else's
girl friend) for fifteen minutes and, unless they know
something that a surprising number of young people
even in this age of enlightened craziness seem not to
know, *voilà!* He is a father. One might almost call it
a *role* in the hay. Unfortunately for millions of children in the world, what it takes to *become* a father
does not automatically provide one with any of the
ingredients required to *be* a father.

God the Father Almighty . . . and the bull down
on the farm. These are the two extremes. The paradox
of fatherhood is that there is truth in both, a mortal
danger in both. So, perspective is needed. But achieving
perspective is like trying to get a bank loan: if you've
got it you don't need it, and if you haven't got it
you're a bad risk. In terms of perspective, most fathers
are bad risks.

I tend to think of fatherhood in three quite different
stages: the father of a child, the father of a youth,
and the father of an adult. This gives each father
three ways to fail, but also two opportunities for redemption.

It all begins in bed, with the act of procreation, when
more seeds are sown than merely the biological. There
are also the seeds of divinity, for there *is* something
godlike about being partly responsible for bringing a
new life into the world. Unfortunately, it is more a
feeling than a becoming. Nothing magic happens to
make the procreator any more divine than he was before. Fertility is the sum total of fatherhood at that

moment. If the man in question happens to have a religious turn of mind, it might occur to him that without the help of God (the real one) he could not have succeeded.

As is usually the case where God is involved, the Devil is right there peddling his influence, setting up shop right in the delivery room. "Hey, man, I see you're into natural childbirth. Good for you! Now don't let your wife tell you that you don't know what she's been through. You've been through it, too. Right?" In my case, because among my contemporaries natural childbirth had long since been forgotten and not yet rediscovered, the Devil stood beside me as we looked together through an antiseptic glass darkly, not absolutely sure which child was mine (which probably pleased God), but, with Mother absent from the scene, leaving me with no rival for the role of creator (which delighted the Devil). Stealing a few lines from Pickering to Henry Higgins in *My Fair Lady*, he whispered in my ear, "You did it! You did it! I always knew you'd do it; *and you did it!*"

Pride! Why not? . . . Because pride just happens to be the father of all sins. What a pity! Just when everything was going so well! First, there is pride of creation. And then, almost simultaneously, pride of possession! The son will struggle for years to try to break free from that possessiveness. Almost before the poor boy has let out his first yelp, the battle lines are drawn. "This is *my* son."

Describing one newborn son, Robert Benchley once said, "He has his father's eyes, his father's nose, and his father's mouth . . . leaving him with a p-r-e-t-t-y blank expression if you ask me." I've seen a lot of fathers like that, handing out cigars, looking fatuous if not blank in their self-satisfaction. Of course, these days Mother doesn't remain "lying in" very long, and that is a help. Father soon gets to share the responsibility and has no more time to hand out cigars. His self-satisfied grin is replaced by the bleary eyes of two A.M. bottles.

Pride of creation and pride of possession, however, do not so easily go away. God made man in his own image, it has been said here and there; and too often it is just this aspect of the Godhead that fathers latch onto. Independent schools and colleges in the northeastern part of the United States prospered for a hundred years or more by nurturing this insidious propensity among their male graduates. I have always hoped that the St. Paul's alumni who entered their sons in their alma mater at birth were at least partly joking, as I also hoped they were when they bought them Harvard T-shirts at the age of two or three with "Class of 19?" on what would someday be a chest. But the only reason it was even partly a joke was that most fathers, fortunately, were too embarrassed to admit outright that they did indeed want their sons to go to school and college where they had gone, in the hope that they would grow up to be as much like their fathers as possible, perhaps even join the family firm, and Father's clubs, and eventually marry one of Father's friends' daughters, and so on, and so on.

Among more modest fathers, pride takes a slightly different turn. They say, in effect, "It is all very well for God to create man in his own image; but I am not entirely pleased with my image, so I shall try for something better." There may be more modesty here, but there is just as much willfulness. Take me, for example.

I have always loved baseball. I never played it very well, but I always wanted to play it well and wanted my sons to play it better than I had. So I started them on it early. Although I batted right-handed, I knew the advantages of batting left-handed, which anyone can do as easily if his father is smart enough to start him out that way. So all my sons were taught from the beginning to bat left-handed. I had also tried catching, but I always closed my eyes whenever the batter swung, which didn't get me very far. I knew, though, that anyone who could catch would have a slight advantage in making teams because hardly anyone naturally likes to catch. It is the most dangerous of all positions. In my infinite wisdom I picked my youngest son to be a catcher, and under my tutelage he actually became good enough to make the junior varsity of his school team. Today he is a professional classical guitarist, with a happy and promising career ahead of him. All he would have had to do was break a few fingers while trying to please his father, and his chosen career would have been next to impossible for him. I shudder when I think of it. Perhaps it was from their mother that my sons learned a certain sense of independence, rather early, that kept them all from ever being any better at baseball than their father and allowed them to grow up to be something other than merely their father's sons.

Of course there are areas in which "Father knows best" is an entirely legitimate idea; but with the world changing so fast, just what does Father know best? Who can be sure what his sons will need to know in order to get along in the world? My father never taught me anything about jumbo jets or television or atom bombs or no-fault insurance or the pill or penicillin; not to mention yoga or Zen or women's lib; let alone withholding tax, or even income tax. Fathers today, like fathers in the past, certainly do know some things

best—mostly about moral laws of cause and effect—
and it is their obligation to pass those things on to
their sons. But the list is not very long; and most fathers have a talent for confusing what Father knows
with what Father wants.

However innocently and charmingly the game begins, it too often has a way of developing into something pretty sinister. As the son moves through child-
hood toward adolescence, the stakes get higher and
higher, or rather what is at stake becomes clearer and
clearer. What is at stake is the son's individual separate
self on the one hand and the father's salvation through
his son on the other. Things don't always come to a
head exactly on the son's thirteenth birthday, as they
did with my son and me; but it is not uncommon for
some sort of crisis to be reached along about then.
Maybe that's why boarding schools have sometimes
prospered, as well as why, during another era, sons
often went to sea. Neither, in my opinion, is altogether
a bad idea. When I went off to boarding school, at the
age of fourteen, my father made a great speech. He
said, "Son, now the name of Verdery is all yours. You
can make anything out of it you want to." As a headmaster I have accepted hundreds of sons who could
hardly wait for their fathers to leave the campus on
opening day; and I have shaken hands with an equal
number of fathers who seemed to be saying, "He's all
yours." By no means, of course, did such partings
mean the end of the war, merely the beginning of a
new phase, with new weapons, and a different battle-
field. Also, as I have already indicated, there is a new
opportunity for redemption.

My own father, who was in many ways a most remarkable and wonderful father, simply flunked round
one altogether. He and my mother parted company

when I was so young that I have no recollection of
his having had much of anything to do with bringing
me up as a child. From the standpoint of the hard work
involved (done mostly by my mother and her father),
this was unforgivable—except that if one believes in
redemption, one believes that nothing is unforgivable.
Inadvertently, I suspect, my father did the one thing
that made redemption possible for him. He took no
credit and no blame for what I was and so managed to
establish a kind of separateness and companionship that
blossomed beautifully later on. But the results could
have been a lot worse in terms of our eventual relationship with each other.

In reading *The Street Where I Live*, by Alan
Lerner, I was struck by certain similarities between his
father and mine. My father, like Mr. Lerner's, was
stagestruck, and not knowing what to do with little boys
when it was his turn to care for them, he did what Mr.
Lerner's father did: he took us to one Broadway show
after another. In fact, I can't figure out how we failed
to meet Alan Lerner—the other little boy in the third
row center. Not having Mr. Lerner's talent, I could
never have written *My Fair Lady*, but at least my
father helped prepare me to be part of Mr. Lerner's
audience. For all his low-key, nonaggressive posture,
my father did succeed in making me somewhat after
his image.

The only other clear memory I have of him as the
father of a child was the day he decided to tell me the
facts of life. I was eleven, and even at that tender age
I sensed the tremendous strain he was under. As I became aware of the subject for discussion, I shared his
agony. It happened that the week before, our teacher
had broached the subject in school, delving as deeply
into it as one would in a class of eleven-year-old boys

and girls. I grasped at this straw and blurted out, before my father had uttered two sentences, "That's all right, Dad, our teacher told us all about it in school last week." My father breathed a sigh of relief and said, "Fine." That was it. The subject was never mentioned again between us.

In round two, as the father of a teen-age son, my father was still not much in the picture. I remember that he occasionally took me to Lawrenceville on a lovely spring day to see a baseball game. (Could he have had the same fixation on that game as I? If so, it was, as in my case, out of frustration rather than accomplishment, for he was no athlete.) As he had gone to Lawrenceville, there was a time when I just assumed that I would be going there too, but his commitment was not to his school, but to his Latin teacher. He had promised himself, while struggling with the ablative absolute in the back of the room (all Verderys always sit in the back of the room), that if he ever had sons, they would have to be taught by that man, the remarkable Charles H. Breed. When the time came for me to go away to school, however, Dr. Breed had left Lawrenceville to become headmaster of Blair Academy. So, one of my brothers and I went to Blair. Could this, too, like the Broadway shows, have been a touch of image making?

I also remember spending some weekends with my father at Princeton. He had made it clear that although he thought it his duty to choose my school, I could certainly choose my college. He would not have thought of making the legendary statement of one father to his son, "You may go to any college in the country; but if you go to Harvard, I'll pay the tuition."

I really think my going to Princeton meant more

to my father than my going to Blair. He had gone there from Lawrenceville, had flunked out midyear of his freshman year, and never gone back. "My only claim to fame," he once said, "was that Eugene O'Neill and I flunked out together, walking hand in hand over the horizon." Cavalier as he was, however, it now seems clear to me that he wanted nothing in the world so much as for one of his sons to go to Princeton and graduate. If so, he deserves credit for never having *imposed* this feeling on me. I went to Princeton with the distinct feeling that it had been my choice. And I did graduate . . . by the skin of my teeth. Some years later I went back to interview some seniors for teaching positions at Wooster. After the interviews, I stopped in at the office of my old friend Howie Stepp, then the registrar, to look up their records. Though the Freedom of Information Act had not yet been passed, he decided to show me my own record. Before handing it to me, he took a look himself.

"Jesus Christ, Verdery, you were dumb," he said. "You were lucky to get out of this place." I *was* lucky. And so was my father, since in some ways his salvation was as much at stake as mine.

The line is thin between a father's hopes for his son and his expectations. Fatherly expectations are heavy things for sons to carry around, whereas hopes, if gently enough expressed, can be a kind of encouragement. During my adolescent years I remember my father's expressing, ever so gently, and not all at once, four hopes for me: that I graduate from Princeton Phi Beta Kappa, that I be a Rhodes scholar, that I win a Guggenheim Fellowship, and that I become governor of Connecticut. There was no obligation . . . just a hint of some goals to shoot for. I have already told by what a wide margin I missed the first, and the second was like unto it. I did once try for a Guggenheim (after my father's death) without any success, and I am still debating about whether or not to try for the fourth.

The contrast between my teen-age sonship of a father and my fatherhood of teen-age sons could hardly be greater. Unlike my father, I was around all the time, and so were they. Furthermore, my turn at fatherhood came in the sixties and early seventies, when all fatherhood was under attack. The consciousness raising on the subject was appalling. One had to *think* about being a father *all the time*. Because my sons and I lived through those years on a school campus, where I spent all of every day dealing with the teen-age sons of other fathers, I had no refuge. My office and my home were all the same to me.

Choosing a secondary school for my sons was not as simple as it had been for my father. There was a school right outside our front door. Although I tried to make it clear to all three boys that none of them had to go there, it was tough to ignore. My oldest son made his choice quickly, with more candor than charm. "It's bad enough having you as a father," he said, "without having you as a headmaster, too." The decision not to go to Wooster was his first venture into the realm of wisdom. It was a good decision, which saved both our lives. So off he went . . . to Blair Academy! I didn't promote it, but I showed it to him and without looking at any other schools he said, "This is it!" It wasn't. The name of Verdery, as my father had put it to me, was still all mine at Blair, and a burden for my son.

The second son wanted to start at Wooster and then go away—which he did, only to come back. With all of my knowledge of the school world and of teen-age boys,

I had not so far done as well as my father. My third son, on the other hand, never considered any school except Wooster and so went there happily for four years. But times had changed again, and there was less heat on fathers and on headmasters and on sons.

Not being a psychiatrist, I am not prepared to say which are the crucial years in the father-son relationship. I am inclined to think that none is, and that all are. But if the adolescent years are not the most crucial, they are certainly the most difficult, for father because of son, for son at least partly because of father. At age sixteen a boy-man is exactly as close to being eight as he is to being twenty-four. The trouble is that he hates everything about himself that is eight and loves, adores, fondles, preens, boasts, exudes, and struts everything about himself that is twenty-four. When his voice cracks he is infuriated, because it is not just his voice but his twenty-four-year-old armor that has cracked, revealing inside the eight-year-old boy, looking very silly because the armor doesn't fit. When his voice stops cracking, other things crack, with the same result. Because being eighteen is exactly as close to being nine as to being twenty-seven, it is a long, hard road for the boy-man and for everyone around him.

These adolescent years have become both the ministry and the educational concern of the better part of my life. What interests me is the delicacy of the teen-age psyche and how you guide one from age thirteen to whatever age proves necessary at the other end of the scale, without destroying the creature and without allowing him (or her) to destroy everyone else. Of course there have been hundreds of times when my patience has worn thin and when I have asked myself why in the world I chose this particular form of hu-

manity to spend my life with. It happens to everyone
in the field. One day I was alarmed to see a colleague
of mine, one of the great teachers, descending the stairs
after a class, looking ashen gray. He had been teaching
for ten years.

"I've just made a horrible discovery," he said. "I'm
allergic to adolescent boys!"

"What happened?"

"They think the sun rises and sets in their own ass-
holes," he said, summarizing the class that he had just
finished teaching. Twenty years later, having learned
more and more patience with each succeeding year, my
friend is still teaching. One of his favorites on today's
faculty is a graduate who was in that very room that
very day. There are rewards. George Bernard Shaw,
whom I greatly revere in his own field, didn't know
what he was talking about when he said, "He who can,
does. He who cannot, teaches." Too often those who
can't teach, try to; but so rare is the gift that I am
inclined to think that those who can teach, should.

Being both a father and a son, I always knew that
one of my jobs as headmaster was to help fathers and
sons form a partnership, to be like a labor-relations
arbitrator, trying not to take sides and trying to see
that negotiations never broke down. Sometimes the job
is made easy by an especially good father. One day I
decided to read through the list in our alumni directory
of the twelve hundred fathers I had known and to pick
out one that seemed to me especially good. Like me, the
one I chose had an adolescent son during the tough
years of the late sixties. The boy was much like his
contemporaries: promising, untested, and insecure
(naturally; what adolescent is not insecure?). The
boy's first year was a little better than average, and he
was selected with eight others to spend his sophomore

year in France. It was a challenge because the program was new and the boys were fifteen and under. This boy's father and mother (he was also blessed with a wonderful mother, but that's another story) were not too keen on the idea. The father said to me, "We spent a long time selecting what we thought would be the very best school we could find for our son to spend four years in, and now you want to send him somewhere else for one-fourth of that time." It was a good point which in my enthusiasm for the program I had never thought of. Nevertheless, he allowed his son to make the choice, and son chose to go. That year passed well, in spite of the fact that the French family turned out to be something less than ideal. Although his own parents went to visit him briefly at Christmas time and observed the situation, they never said anything to me. The father just assumed that his son could handle it, which he did.

The son's last two years at Wooster happened to be the two most difficult years for boarding schools generally that I have ever known. The shaking of the foundations that had been felt on college campuses throughout the land had begun to be felt on school campuses as well. Drugs arrived. Authority was threatened. Philosophical assumptions were challenged. That a large part of the unrest was simply a question of "Monkey see, monkey do"—younger brother in school mimicking big brother in college—did not help any. What I remember most vividly is how unhappy everyone was! And, of course, under pressure, everyone was blaming everyone else. The schools blamed the parents and the parents blamed the school, and the children blamed both. Trust was undermined.

Wooster was not immune to any of these difficulties, and neither was the son of my selected father. Except for drugs, there were no issues that were new; but there was a heightening of intensity about everything, an extraordinary strain in human relationships. Maybe one reason my star father looked to me so much like a star is that he performed so normally and naturally in an atmosphere that was anything but normal and natural. He was calm and he was patient and he resisted the temptation to assign blame.

What this man did was trust his son, *before* he had proved himself trustworthy and *after* he had proved himself in some ways untrustworthy. That is the sum of my evidence that he was a remarkable father. How peculiar! Don't all fathers, almost, trust their sons? If you ask any of us, we will all say yes, of course. But most of us just don't know what the word *trust* means. It is something that, by its very definition, is offered before there is evidence that it is deserved and then again after there may be evidence that it is not deserved. *It has nothing to do with deserving.* It is like the marriage vows, which read, in effect, *not* "I will be faithful to you if you are faithful to me," but simply, "I will be faithful to you."

Allan Heely, of Lawrenceville, once made a speech to the trustees and faculty of another school that was about to take on one of his young teachers as its headmaster. He said, "I expect you to support him when he is right . . . and also when he is wrong." That, too, is what my selected father did for his son.

In writing about this man, I have been surprised at how unspectacular he seems on the printed page. I even went over the list again to see if I couldn't find someone more colorful. But eventually it dawned on me that a good father needn't be either spectacular or colorful. Indeed, what it takes is three qualifications that by their very nature are most often not spectacular or colorful, namely, trust, support . . . and love.

The third stage of fatherhood, being the father of an adult son, is often ignored. It is tempting to believe that it doesn't really matter because the game is over. It is a little like the last singles in a Davis Cup tennis match, with one team ahead 4–0. Who cares who wins, since it can't affect the outcome? But I see it as the last chance for a lot of fathers to redeem themselves, and thus as obviously of some importance to their sons.

The question of when a son is an adult could be argued until the bulls come home; but the law of the land has a simple answer—age eighteen. So why argue? Why should we not begin to treat our sons as men the day the law says that they are men?

That implies trust—the trust of an adult toward an adult. A few years ago I was asked to give the commencement address at the Kent School. As sort of a joke, but to make this very serious point, I made a "modest proposal" to all the fathers present. I suggested that they express their trust of their adult sons by simply giving them the price of college (or whatever they had planned to contribute toward college) in cold cash on that very graduation day from Kent. "Son, I was planning to contribute $8,000 a year for the next four years toward your college. Take the $32,000 now and do what you want. There won't be any more; but I trust you to do what you think is best for you, with the money and with the next four years of your life." The fathers in the audience all groaned audibly, the sons all stood up and cheered, and everyone else burst out laughing. Why? Because, of course, the fathers did not yet trust their sons *that* far; and because the sons honestly considered themselves utterly trustworthy.

Although my modest proposal was a histrionic device, it nevertheless served to symbolize the importance of money in the relationship between fathers and adult sons. It is too late for the stick, so money becomes the carrot, all that is left of a father's authority, control, and influence (except for such abstract things as love, respect, admiration, and so forth). Sometimes money is used in the form of an allowance that goes on and on and on. I know one father who is still giving his forty-year-old son an allowance, thinking that he is being big-hearted.

One of my favorite fathers gave his children everything that he was planning to leave them well before he died because he wanted to see them enjoy it and because he didn't want to see them waiting around for him to die. Maybe one reason my father and I got along so well was that he didn't have a red cent. His funeral expenses were paid for by the Hod Carriers' Union, which he had joined shortly after flunking out of Princeton and to which he had paid dues all his life.

The trouble with money is that it is such a serious thing. We don't object too much if our sons want to drop out of college for a year. If they want to live with a girl friend out of wedlock, we may not like it, but we don't say too much. Whatever emotional patterns may be upset we assume can be straightened out later. But money! We *can't* let our sons blow a few thousand dollars. It almost seems as though money is the final measure—the measure of responsibility, the measure of maturity, and so the measure of trust.

The important thing for fathers of adults to realize is that they must *let go*. The time has come (always sooner than we think) to move to the sidelines, and not as a coach, but just as part of the cheering section, applauding victories and commiserating over defeats, dressing a wound now and then, but never sending in any plays. Sometimes the letting go can even include a little push. There are fathers of adults who could take lessons from mother robins. When my oldest son turned twenty-one (the legal age of manhood at that time), I handed him a savings bank book I had started when he was four. "Here. This is now yours. I am no longer your legal guardian." Half joking and half serious, he said, handing the book back. "Please, Dad, won't you be my legal guardian a *little* longer?" I refused.

My father, as I have said, redeemed himself in the third round of fatherhood. Circumstances helped. My mother died during my senior year in college, and the following fall I found myself at Union Seminary, in New York City, where my father lived. We immediately became firm friends and remained so until his death twenty years later. Since my grandfather had done all the spanking in the earlier years (with a razor strop), and my mother had done most of the rest of the chastising, there were no scars from the past in my relationship with my father. Of course, this gave him an unfair advantage vis-à-vis most fathers, but at least he made the most of it.

He was a short, round man who walked with a quick, almost dancing step, his head high and his eyes straight forward, as though he were trying to see over the horizon. He loved to laugh, and he loved making other people laugh. He particularly enjoyed what he called a "nifty," a fast answer that hit the mark. He had been brought up in Flushing, New York, next to the Barrymores, and he and John had been boyhood friends. Toward the end of his life, while walking down Fifth Avenue, he ran into John Barrymore, who recognized my father first, though he had not seen him in more than fifty years. He approached my father (whose nickname was Jack), put out his hand, and said, "Your name is Jack. But I can't remember your last name." Shaking the proffered hand, my father replied, "Your name is Barrymore, but I can't remember your first name." That made them both laugh, and they stopped at the nearest bar to have a drink together—which they were both good at. That was, I think, my father's niftiest nifty.

He shared my excitement about Union Seminary just as if he were going there with me. In fact, one day I invited him to join me for a lecture by Reinhold Niebuhr. The theology escaped him, but not the performance. Niebuhr had a delivery like a machine gun. He wore an academic gown that flowed in the breeze caused by his constant sailing back and forth in front of the podium. Every now and then he would flash a very handsome profile as he looked off into space, lost in thought. Then he would whip on his large horn-rimmed glasses to read something to us. He was one of the few lecturers I have ever heard who justified the lecture method. In his hands it was a creative thing. It *was* a performance. "My God," said my father when the lecture was over, "he's a cross between John Barrymore and Bobby Clark" (a comedian of the time who wore painted-on glasses).

As the father of an adult son, my father was not above finding fault. But he did it so gently. Once, after I had become a headmaster, a friend of the family did me a favor and I forgot to thank her. My father wrote me a letter suggesting that I do so, and in the letter were two enclosures, with no reference to either of them. One was a telegram from my grandfather to Woodrow Wilson, dated July 8, 1919. The other was a thank-you note from the president, dated July 10,

1919. My father knew I was going to tell him how busy I had been. Now, both the letter and the telegram are framed on the wall of my office.

What my father had in his later years was humor and perspective (which are surely related), and a lot of selflessness, and a lot of love. I was well over forty when he died, a time when a man really ought not to need a father anymore. But the deep sense of loss that I felt indicated that a father is a nice thing to have around, at any age. For his funeral his host of friends gathered from far and wide. Making and keeping friends was his greatest single talent. We sat around the tiny living room of his Vermont house, where he had retired, waiting for the clans to gather, and swapped Jack Verdery stories for two days. I think I never heard so much laughter in all my life.

Recently my sister came across a letter my father wrote to my mother just after they were married. It describes an incident that took place about 1916. He was working in a shipyard in California, and he and a friend were driving from the shipyard into town when they came upon a couple by the side of the road with a flat tire. It seems that they were on their way to the hospital, where she was about to deliver herself of a baby. And time was running very short. So my father and friend took the young lady and rushed her to the nearest hospital, wondering from her wailing if they would get there in time. The following description illustrates my father's sense of humor as well as his love of the stage.

(Enter Jack, approaches desk with the bored expression of a professional father.)
Jack: Good afternoon, can you take a confinement case?

Matron: We're sorry, but we're full.

Jack: So is the woman I have outside in the automobile.

Matron: Well, I'm sure I don't know where we can put her.

Jack: Then you can appreciate how I feel.

Matron (laughing): Who is she?

Jack: I don't see what that has to do with it, but she is going to be somebody's mother in about ten minutes. Frankly, I don't know who she is, but I have diagnosed the case beyond peradventure.

(Matron phones ward 30, says a lot of technical things, hangs up phone.)

Matron: Well, we'll take her.

Jack: Thank you. I'll do the same for you someday.

Matron: If you'll tell me where you got her, I won't require any more.

Jack: Your question is a fair one.

(Matron and Jack go offstage arm in arm.)

Most fathers of a son are also husbands of wives, as well as doctors, lawyers, merchants, chiefs. Some of them are also fathers of daughters and other sons. They have friends outside the family, as well as hobbies and interests outside their careers. It is also not uncommon for a father to like to be by himself now and then, alone with his thoughts or his prayers. In short, fathers of sons have things in their lives besides their sons, just as sons have things in their lives besides their fathers. How well a father keeps his responsibility to his son in balance with his many other responsibilities and personal needs is an important measure of how good a father he is.

I think of two fathers whom I knew very well. One was a world-famous public servant. People spoke of him in awe, not only because of his professional accomplishments, but as much for his voluntary contributions to the good of society. In spite of his brillance and fame, he was a modest man who seemed to have trouble believing that he was as important as he was. If he had a weakness, it was as a father and a husband. Generous beyond belief to the claims of the world on his time and attention, he seemed to have nothing left over for his family.

His son bore the same name and lived, from his first day at school till the day he died of cirrhosis of the liver, with the question "Are you the son of the famous Mr. So-and-so?" Sons have survived famous and pre-occupied fathers time and again throughout history. Some, like Mr. Pitt the Younger and several members of the Adams family, have become famous themselves. But it is not an easy assignment, and this man's son, who was my close friend, couldn't handle it and so eventually drank himself to death. It wasn't his father's fault; and yet, if he had spent a little more time and a little more of his emotional self on his son, things might have been different.

The other father never finished high school, and his career consisted simply of earning a living however he could. He once said to me, "I never had a chance to amount to anything because I always had too many responsibilities." What he meant by responsibilities was being a father and being a husband. At both he was superb—selfless, graceful, and always available. He had three sons, the three most remarkable sons to come out of the same family that I have ever known. One graduated from Princeton, one from Yale, and one from Harvard, two of them Phi Beta Kappa—a neat trick in itself, but only the beginning of what one might say about these three rather exceptional brothers. Two are already well into distinguished careers, and the third is on his way. But beyond education and careers, they share a common spiritual quality that must have come from somewhere. Of course, they owe a lot to a very strong and decisive mother, as well as to sheer luck and their own initiative; but there can be no denying the debt to a father who in a sense had made a decision that *they* would be his career.

I do not think that either of these examples of fatherhood represents the ideal. A man has got to have a life of his own, and he owes the society that is outside his home a fair share of his talent, energy, and good will. But it would be good if that debt to society could be paid without resulting in the destruction of his son. A father's absenteeism is not a crime in itself, nor is preoccupation with affairs outside the family; and omnipresence is not automatically a virtue, any more than is undivided attention. There are the proverbial Little League fathers who give their sons a great deal of their time and attention, often more attention than the son can handle. They are not necessarily good fathers; in fact, sometimes they are perfectly terrible fathers. There are big-time business executives, on the other hand, who may be away from home for days and weeks and even while at home be burdened with bulging briefcases and urgent phone calls that must be made. I have been a houseguest of many such men and have watched them function in their homes. Some of them are wonderful fathers. A proper balance can be achieved.

The answer is in the quality of love, which unfortunately may introduce a whole new set of questions. When asked his advice on how to bring up children, Robert Oppenheimer, a father with more than a little

in the way of outside distractions, replied, "Pour in
the love!" That is beautiful, particularly coming from
such a man. But what does it mean? Surely David
loved Absalom as much as any father has ever loved a
son. His cry of anguish at the news of his son's death
is as heartrending as any I know: "O my son Absalom,
my son, my son Absalom! Would I had died instead
of you. O Absalom, my son, my son Absalom!" Yet
David's love was demanding and self-serving. It was a
love that made him capable of inviting Absalom back
to his home city of Jerusalem—forgiven for having
led an insurrection against his father—but also of
refusing to see him for two years. The father of the
Prodigal Son displayed a better quality of love. Having given his son his total inheritance when the boy
was still very young, and the boy having squandered it
and returned home empty-handed and hungry, a total
failure, his father *ran* out to meet him, kissed him, and
forgave him.

St. Paul, who was neither a father nor a husband and
at times was even (in my opinion) a most difficult person, nevertheless managed to identify the qualities of
love as clearly as anyone ever has. The spaces between
the phrases are designed to invite one to think long
and hard about the implications of each.

"Love is patient and kind. . . . Love is not jealous
or boastful. . . . It is not arrogant or rude. . . .
Love does not insist on its own way. . . . It is not ir-
ritable or resentful. . . . It does not rejoice at wrong,
but rejoices in the right. . . . Love bears all things
. . . believes all things . . . hopes all things . . . en-
dures all things. . . . Love never ends."

E. B. White is one of my very favorite writers, but
he nevertheless wrote the most disturbing single sentence I have ever read: "There is no such thing as a

happy ending." That bothered me for months after I first read it. It seemed to undermine so much that I have held dear all my life, just because it seemed, even under close examination, to be so irrefutably true. I don't *want* to believe that there is no such thing as a happy ending! Here is the escape clause, the non-catch-twenty-two: "Love never ends."

Maybe that's all the father of a son needs to know.

Black and White Is Beautiful

SINCE the word *integration* and the word *integrity* come from the same stem, it is obvious that where there is prejudice, there can be no integration; and that where there is integrity, there can be no prejudice. In 1943, when I first came to Wooster, there had never been a black student in our school; but neither had there been in any other boarding school in Connecticut, nor had there ever been one in my university alma mater, Princeton, nor in fact, had I personally ever known but one black person of my own age (a seminary classmate). And yet the protestation that was most often heard in this context was "Of course, we have no prejudice against them." How comforting it was, in those days, to have no sense of sin! Prejudice, it is said, is blind; and like most other sins, it is also deaf and dumb.

Sometimes truth dawns. As with the rising sun, there is at first nothing but a vague hint of light. Then that light spreads, pushing back the darkness—but slowly.

It is quite a while before one can see by that light, and then again a while before the full burst of the sun. The Connecticut Headmasters Association used to meet regularly twice a year, to talk about shoes and ships and sealing wax, and cabbages, and kings—that is to say, the pros and cons of early football practice, how much we paid our chefs, and if there were not some way that we could integrate . . . the dates of our spring vacations. It was not until 1946, eighty years after the end of the Civil War, that I remember the subject of the racial integration of our student bodies to have been brought up for the first time. And then it was mostly for the purpose of reassuring ourselves that we were really not prejudiced. "We would be glad to have a Negro student in our school," one man said. "It's just that no qualified Negro has ever applied." It would be still some years before there would be enough morning light in our minds to see that maybe some people don't want to crash parties to which they have never been invited. One man, whom I greatly admired in other respects, said to me, "You know, I live in constant dread every fall that when we come down to play you in football, you will have a Negro on your team."

The story of the racial integration of the independent schools of New England is not a very exciting story, or a very dramatic one, when compared with the march on Selma, or James Meredith's entrance into the University of Mississippi. It has no martyrs, like Martin Luther King, Jr., or Jonathan Daniels. It hasn't even any heroes. And yet, as a background for studying the nature of prejudice, it is as good as any. The elements are all there, and all at work. In fact, the very lack of drama and heroism and martyrdom in some ways makes it easier to understand at least some aspects of prejudice. Prejudice isn't always passionate.

Something I wrote some time ago on this subject attracted the attention of a former student of mine, H. Brandt Ayers. Brandy, as he was called in his school days, is the editor and publisher of the *Anniston Star*, "Alabama's Largest Home-Owned Newspaper." When Brandy attended Wooster, sent there by a farseeing father who thought his son should know some other part of the country before settling back in the South, the school had not yet enrolled its first black student. In fact, the first black ever to spend a night in a Wooster dorm was Brandy's father's chauffeur, Eli, who had driven the family up to Brandy's graduation and was refused a bed in the local inn. Having read what I had written, Brandy responded by writing a column in his paper on the subject (just twenty-five years after that graduation): "What struck me most," he wrote, "was the universality of the experience: A Connecticut boarding school had a common experience with Alabama public school principals, headmasters of progressive Southern private schools, even with Bear Bryant and University of Alabama basketball coach C. M. Newton." Though the testimony comes from an unusually loyal alumnus and personal friend, I am encouraged to repeat myself.

The prejudice that kept Wooster an all-white school for the first thirty years of its history was of the non-passionate variety. We just lived happily, sleeping in the dark, with no hint of dawn breaking. In spite of the fact that we were a church school, with plenty of hints in hymns and lessons and prayers *every single day*, we just didn't think anything was wrong! What caused us finally to begin to see I cannot say. Probably a combination of things—Jackie Robinson, maybe; or perhaps simply what St. Paul called "the fullness of time." What I do know is that when the light did begin to dawn and we began to see, nothing much happened right away. It would still be *ten years* before Wooster would enroll its first black student, and we were ahead of most.

Prejudice is like an artichoke. You have to remove leaf after leaf after leaf before you get to the heart of the matter; and when you finally do, you find it full of prickles that have to be cut out before you reach the heart. Prejudice is personal and insidious; it is harmful and a barrier against truth and justice; it is impossible to cut out completely, and so keeps growing back. But like an artichoke, prejudice starts out innocently enough. When we finally started dealing with our prejudice about blacks in our school, we really enjoyed the exercise; it made us feel warm inside.

For us the first leaf of the artichoke was the simple acknowledgment that it was not right for us to be an all-white school and that we had to do something about it. We had to *not* be an all-white school, no matter what that might involve. We came to realize that that was a huge step forward from "We would be glad to have a Negro in our school, but no qualified Negro has applied."

The phrase "Black is beautiful" was undoubtedly coined to contrast with practically every ad on TV and in every slick magazine of twenty years ago, which all seemed to cry out, "White is beautiful." What we at last decided was not that white is beautiful and black is also beautiful, but that black and white is beautiful. To be integrated thus became an urgent priority, and we could at last give up the practice of explaining why we were not.

Several friends who have read some of the things that I have written on this subject have criticized me for what they call my breast beating, for overemphasizing the question of guilt, for my *mea culpa* tone. They argue, or rather the Devil in them argues, that I was no worse than anybody else in those days, that "times were different, that's all." I have to argue now, because their tone is part of the story that is to be told, that I disagree. I do not believe that integration to the point of integrity can ever be achieved in any society, however large or small, without some confession of guilt for the past. There is a difference between being forgiven (which can only take place after there has been a confession) and being excused. To say, "I didn't know any better" is very different from saying, "I didn't know any better, so you can't blame me. . . . It wasn't my fault."

It is a measure of our guilt that when we finally got around to making a decision about admitting our first black students, the climate of opinion was such that there was neither much argument nor even much discussion. That was in 1954, ten years after the thought had first been introduced to our collective mind. And then, because we were so fearful of not getting things off on the right foot, we took two more years of searching to find "just the right boys." One of our criteria was that they (we had agreed that we would start with two) should not be outstanding athletes *because we didn't want them to be too conspicuous!* Picture the opening day of school, in September 1956, lines forming before the registration desk, seniors showing new students and their parents around the campus, a picnic on the front lawn—and our first two black boys ever, *looking inconspicuous.*

One of those first two black boys was Camilo Marquez, and he is today a distinguished psychiatrist in New York City. But at age fifteen he was a cool cat who thought that the whole idea of Wooster School becoming integrated was something of a joke. It had not yet occurred to us that he might have come from a school that was integrated (which he did), so that the novelty was only for us, not for him. He walked around the campus with an amused smirk, wearing a scotch plaid cap, with the brim just barely above his eyebrows, so that he had to tip his head back to look at you. As I would pass him on the campus, he would wave at me by making a semicircle in the air, his palm flat, look out from under his cap, smile, and say, "Hi." What he seemed to be saying was "How you doin' with your integration?" When he came back for his twentieth class reunion, he was still smiling, and even though I count him as one of my very close friends, I am still not sure what he thinks.

An early problem to be dealt with was the question of roommates. Among the Connecticut Headmasters, most of whom had also achieved virtue at about this time, there were two schools of thought: they *must* room together, and they *may not* room together. Wooster took the latter position, with secret feelings of moral superiority over those who took the former, not realizing until some years later that both positions were wrong. Another leaf.

The next issue was numbers, which served to clarify the original question of motivation. Why were we integrating our school? Was it because the law would get after us if we didn't? Was it to give a better chance in life to a handful of young men handicapped by the color of their skin? Was it because it was the Christian thing to do? Or was it for educational reasons, in order to have a healthier community? Though it is dangerous to attribute motive in retrospect, I believe that our initial motive was Christian and that later on, much later on, we discovered the virtues and the educational advantages of a multiracial community. The National Scholarship and Service Fund for Negro Students, long involved in helping young blacks on the college level, got into the independent school field just as soon as there were any indications that the schools were ready and willing, thus underlining the poverty of the old argument, "No qualified . . ." and so on. If one wanted numbers, all one had to do was ask. We asked, and so had four black students our second year and six the year after that. We felt very virtuous.

But what is the right number? When we got to six, I thought six was the right number. I remember that summer going off for my vacation, with the school more or less full for the fall, but with a couple of spots to be filled by the director of admissions. I also remember my feelings of uneasiness when I learned that he had filled one of those spots with another black boy. Seven? That's too many. But what was the trouble? Was I nervous? Was I afraid? Of what? Or was I just annoyed that someone else had made the decision, the decision that numbers really didn't matter?

We learned to live with numbers, and to like it. Once we had six blacks all in the same class (most of them rooming together, by choice). When they were juniors, the time came to elect what we called the Fifth Form Council. The method of election was primitive. The class was called together, and people simply nominated candidates from the floor, at which point the nominees were asked to leave the room so that discussion could be freer. To my horror, all six black boys were nominated, and all left the room. What frightened me was not the prospect that they would be elected to fill all five positions on the council, but that, with an all-white voting bloc left in the room, *none* of them would be elected. I should have had no fears. The younger we are the less prejudice we have. The question of race was discussed very briefly, and then the class proceeded to elect those whom they thought would be the five best, one of whom turned out to be a black. Afterward, one of the black losers came up to me and said, not angrily and not bitterly, "Wouldn't it have been something if five of us had been elected? We'd have made the cover of *Ebony!*"

To learn anything of value in a school about the insidious nature of prejudice, it is necessary to have numbers of black students. Numbers present problems, and the solving of problems is part of the essence of education. Numbers represent a threat, and if you are never threatened, you never learn that the heart of the artichoke is full of little prickles. Any school that has enough blacks might end up with a black basketball team, though probably not a black hockey team. So the white basketball player is threatened, whereas the white hockey player is not. What a salubrious atmosphere in which to teach both of them something about the nature of prejudice!

Some people cannot be expected to understand. I was showing a parent of a prospective student around the school, and we came into the dining room during lunch. He turned to a table of all black boys and said, "Do you allow black tables?" Thinking fast, but accurately in this case, I said, "That's not a black table. That's the basketball team." But God is good. And that year we just happened to have one white boy on the basketball team, and one black boy on the hockey team, which amused everybody.

It was inevitable with numbers, and with the nature of the atmosphere throughout the land, that we should eventually be faced with the problem of militancy. It hit us late and very mildly, but it was nevertheless a new element to be coped with. This was dramatized for me by the story of a white boy from Virginia whom I shall call Dick Stevens. Dick came from one of the "first families," which was at least liberal enough to have sent him to Wooster. After his first year, Dick signed up to room with a black friend for the following year. When he went home for the summer, he reported this fact, as casually as he could, to his family. His father, knowing his son to be something of a rebel (not after the manner of his ancestors, but after the manner of the young of his day), assumed that the boy was just trying to pick a fight and so paid no attention to him. Toward the end of the summer, Dick realized that his father had not believed him and so repeated the statement. At that his father called me and asked me to do something about it. On the opening day of school, when he found out that I had not, he badgered me in my office. "You know, of course," he said, "that we're not prejudiced. But the friends we have at home are just not ready for this sort of thing; and if Dick were to bring his roommate home over a vacation, it would be a disaster for everyone."

"You'll have to tell that to Dick," I said. "Here we have just two rules about roommates. They must be in the same class, and they must both be in favor of the arrangement. Beyond that we are not willing to interfere." We called the boy in and his father gave him pretty much the same speech he had just given me, though, I noted, in a much milder form. The boy listened intently and politely, with his jaw slightly protruding. When his father finished, Dick said, "Father, your home is your home. And I wouldn't think of bringing anyone into it that you don't want. But here at school my room is my home, and I'll room with anyone I wish."

If that were the end of the story, it would be beautiful. The two boys got along fine that year, but the following year Dick went to France on the Wooster French program. And when he came back, the atmosphere at Wooster, and in America, had changed. A new black boy from a big-city ghetto had entered, and he was militant. He took it out on Dick (whom he hardly knew) unmercifully on the football field. Dick, who was tough enough to take care of himself, just didn't understand. Rather than being angry, he was bewildered and hurt. So were many well-meaning white people at that time, including myself. The only thing different about Dick was that he had been out of the country for a year and hadn't seen it coming.

White reaction to black militancy is not difficult to understand. When one takes a moral step forward in dealing with others, one cannot help but feel a touch of pride and self-satisfaction, and look immediately (subconsciously or otherwise) for some sort of reward. The most natural and common is gratitude. When I begin to treat my neighbor better than I used to, I'd at least like him to notice it, and to let me know that he has noticed it, and maybe even to thank me. At Wooster we had gone to great pains to become an integrated school; we had gambled our reputation and our very existence; we had begged for money from all kinds of sources to make it possible; we had dispensed a lot of that money directly to the well-being of individual black young people; we had, we thought, thereby presented them with possibilities for their lives that could not have come to pass without our help. In the early years all of this had been rewarded just as we had wanted. The blacks were dutiful and grateful, appreciative, even admiring.

Then suddenly, they began to bite the hand that we thought was feeding them. They began to snarl, to group together almost to the point of excluding everyone who was not black. They formed a Black Student Union. They asked for dances for blacks only; and at mixed dances they insisted on at least as much soul music as rock. If a black boy was seen dating or even paying too much attention to a white girl, he was reprimanded by his black brothers.

Reactions varied. Dick Stevens's was mild. Almost without exception, the most extreme reactions came not from the students, but from members of the faculty. No one had yet realized that to *insist* on gratitude and appreciation, which in effect was what we were doing, is degrading. It undermines dignity, is just another way of keeping the social scale out of balance.

In Provence some years ago I made a speech to thank our French families for having had Wooster students in their homes for a year. The speech had to be in French, and wanting to show off a bit, I thought I'd throw in a few words of Provençal. But when I asked a friend who spoke the language what the Provençal word for *thank you* was, he replied, "There is no such word in Provençal. The Provençaux are a proud people. If they are grateful, they express it in action; but they would think it degrading to say the words. You know," he continued, "there is also no word for *thank you* in French. The word *merci* is a medieval word, originating in the time of lords and serfs. The lord could do all sorts of gracious things for his serfs, if he chose. But there was no way the serfs could return the favor and so lighten the debt. Debt is a heavy burden, and when it gets too much, you cry for mercy. 'Don't do anything more for me. I can't stand it. Have mercy!' " *Faveur* is the first definition given in the French dictionary for the word *merci*. The heart of the rise of black militancy in America, and in our school, is to be found, I believe, in this concept of an indebtedness of which gratitude is the acknowledgment. The whole point of the civil rights movement was *rights*, not debts. "Biting the hand that feeds them" is a dead giveaway as an expression. "What, no thanks?" No! Only nonnegotiable demands! Cassius Clay and Lew Alcindor changed their names. Why? Because they were tired of being beholden.

What helped me most at that point in my life was reading the *Autobiography of Malcolm X*. As a white, and as a Christian, I could only feel shame and guilt while reading that book. A dinner partner not long ago told me that she thought guilt was the most unproductive of human emotions, that any psychiatrist would tell me the same thing. I think she was confusing guilt with a guilt complex, or with feelings of guilt. Guilt is not an emotion. It is a fact, or else it is not a fact. Feelings of guilt, whether justified or not, are proper areas for psychiatrists and psychologists to deal with. The fact of guilt—or innocence—is something to be dealt with by a court, or by a confessional booth, or by a conscience. If one *is guilty* of something, the only way out is to confess and to make amends. Reading the *Autobiography of Malcolm X* made me realize that I have some guilt to share. Blithely to have gone through four years of Princeton University, for example, knowing perfectly well that no black had ever been allowed in, and not for one minute ever to have let that bother me, was to have made a personal contribution, however small, to a condition in our land that caused Malcolm X to write the way he did, live the way he did, and die the way he did. It is not enough to say that the time was not right, or that I had plenty of company among my friends, or that "nobody was thinking along those lines in those days." Malcolm X was. I don't think this is a complex on my part. I think it is a fact, and that the only way out for me is to acknowledge the fact and do what I can to make amends.

It is easy to believe, though I do not think it is true, that a great deal of black militancy was *designed expressly* to make white people angry, and thereby cause them to show their true feelings. After reading *Malcolm X*, I decided that no black militant, even if he spat in my face, was going to catch me in that trap. I was bound and determined that I was going to understand black militancy and learn to cope with it in such a way that reconciliation would always be possible.

A Frenchman who knew nothing much about race relations in America, and a black American whom I never met, combined to teach me something. Another leaf.

One September afternoon in 1980, at a gathering of Wooster parents seeing their children off at Kennedy Airport for the school's year-in-France program, I was talking to the father of the only black boy in the group. He told me that he had given his fifteen-year-old son just two books to take with him for the year. One of them was the *Autobiography of Malcolm X*.

Going back to 1970, there was on the Wooster campus that new tension. It was never very extreme, but it was new. There was among some whites—students and faculty alike—a feeling that ranged from bewilderment to bitterness to anger over the disappearance of gratitude and the appearance of what they called "arrogance" (another loaded word) on the part of the blacks. It was as though the rules had been changed in the middle of the game.

Then one day a miracle took place. The black students asked if they could conduct a chapel service for the whole school on the subject of black awareness, to try to explain to the whites what it means to be black. The school chapel, with the pews facing each other, is just big enough to accommodate the whole school community, but in an atmosphere (at least on that day) of uncomfortable intimacy. The "service" started out on a tone obviously designed to shock and make trouble. There were poetry readings, some written by the students themselves and some taken from published literature of the moment, all filled with obscenities and crudities. Then there was a speech, in the same vein. That was followed by what was introduced as a question period, during which some of the black students paraded up and down the center aisle, walking right up to the questioner and staring at him while he asked his question. This question period was preceded by a gesture that seemed ominous at the time. One of the black boys walked the whole length of the chapel, exuding arrogance, closed the doors, then turned around and faced the congregation, indicating that it was time for the questions to begin. It seemed clear that in his mind the whole exercise would last just as long as he wanted it to. That turned out to be about forty-five minutes.

The miracle was that during that whole time, not one white person, boy or girl, faculty or student, for one moment lost his or her composure or courtesy. One could only assume from the nature and tone of the questions that the entire white community had taken the black community at their word, that they were there simply to learn something about what it was like to be black. Little by little the atmosphere became more and more relaxed, the courtesy was more and more returned from the other side, until finally the exercise actually began to be boring. At that point a boy by the name of José stood up in the back row and was called on. José is a Chicano. Some Chicanos look more Spanish than Indian; but José looked almost like a full-blooded Indian, with high cheekbones and long, straight, jet-black hair. He said, simply, "I don't know what you're talking about. I'm not black. And I'm not white." Then he started to head for the exit. Everybody sort of shrugged his shoulders, looked at each other, and got up and followed him out of the chapel.

Black militancy died that day on the Wooster campus, and so far it has never returned.

Sometime well before that famous chapel service, a new truth had begun to dawn: black and white may be beautiful, but it is not beautiful enough. In the chapel that day there were, in addition to blacks and whites, Chicanos, Puerto Ricans, and Orientals, as well as some Arabs and some Jews. It would be wonderful to be able to say that all came to pass by plan, motivated by a clear and early vision of a thoroughly racially and religiously mixed society as the ideal educational community. We have that conviction now, but honesty would insist that it came about only partly by plan and conviction—arrived at very slowly and tentatively —and partly by accident.

I think the first Jew was admitted with no conscious plan, and I have no idea who he was. The Arabs came because there is a large Arab community in the area where the school is located. The first Puerto Rican was admitted as part of the black program, with no forethought. The Chicanos, like the blacks, came through a carefully thought-out plan. The first Japanese American came during World War II, from one of those camps that Americans like to forget. Under the circumstances he should have caused more of a stir than the first blacks; but he didn't cause any at all.

One day I found myself watching the girls' varsity volleyball team playing one of our rivals. We were losing, and I started to look around for something to cheer me up. Suddenly, I noticed that the opposing team, all six of them, were blond with blue eyes. Then I looked at our team—one black, one Chinese, one Arab, one Jew, one French exchange student, and one WASP. "Ah," I said to myself (and, of course, later on to anyone who would listen), "that's the name of the game!" And then I remembered "ethnic pass catching." Ethnic pass catching was a game invented by our very imaginative football coach the fall before. The season was a dismal one, moving from one defeat to another, each by a larger score. In order to keep up the morale of the team through the long weeks of practice, he ended each session with a contest in catching passes, by ethnic groups, the score kept throughout the season, and an award to be presented at the banquet. (Incidentally, the Jews won and the blacks came in last . . . another leaf.)

Whether by accident or by design, or a combination of both, Wooster School had been transformed from an all-white community into one of the most thoroughly racially integrated boarding schools in the country. Naturally, we take pride in that fact, though our pride is tempered by the knowledge that it took more than twenty years to accomplish.

There is still prejudice in our school, even racial prejudice. As humans, we have it ingrained in our beings. There is no way to prevent ourselves, sometimes, from making instant judgments about others. If we don't know them, we stereotype them. The typical Jew is hard-working, money-grubbing, obsessed with the education of his children, socially pushy. The typical black is lazy, morally loose, given to violence, arrogant, and unfriendly to non-blacks. The typical WASP is a snob, protective of his own kind, desirous of insulating himself with exclusive clubs and schools and real-estate holdings and marital taboos. The typical southern white is a redneck, his northern counterpart a self-satisfied liberal.

As people get to know each other as individuals, there is a chance that they will learn that all Jews, all blacks, all WASPs, and all whites are *not* typical. That is a step forward. It is not possible for a student to live long in a community like Wooster and not know at least that much. And to have taught that much has been worth the effort. But prejudice disappears only when one comes to realize that there is no such thing as typical. All typecasting is superficial, unreal, and unfair. Only in theory have most of us ever been able to get this far. Prejudice persists.

One day I was to perform a wedding at St. James Episcopal Church, on Madison Avenue and 71st Street. On the same day I attended the funeral of the father of one of our black students, in Harlem. The funeral was in the morning, and I took our senior prefect along with me to represent the student body. His name was Bernie Beal. He was black and lived not far from where the funeral was to take place. We parked our car on Lenox Avenue, near the funeral home. I had on a dark suit, a black homburg, and a black chesterfield coat. I was carrying a small suitcase with my vestments in it for the wedding. As we got out of the car, Bernie, being polite, offered to carry my suitcase. I almost let him; and then suddenly I realized what a picture we would make, walking down Lenox Avenue together. I said, "No, Bernie, not here!" He looked at me, puzzled for an instant, then we both burst out laughing, Bernie actually slapping his thigh like an old-time comedian. In the nick of time we had avoided arousing the animosity of prejudice; but we must have seemed an odd couple even so, as we entered the funeral home, where it turned out that I was the only white in a congregation of more than four hundred people. At the wedding that afternoon there were also about four hundred people—but no blacks.

My friend Donald Schwartz left teaching at Wooster to teach for eight years in a drug rehabilitation center in Harlem. He became known to everyone in the area, and, although in his modesty he would deny it, he became something of a local hero. One evening that same Bernie, whom Donald had taught at Wooster, came to call on him after work. They were standing together on the street corner, waiting for Donald's bus. It was ten-thirty P.M. Bernie said, "Mr. Schwartz, doesn't it ever make you nervous to be out on the streets of Harlem alone at night?" Donald said, "No, Bernie. You're the one who should be nervous. This is my part of Harlem."

Bernie now works in his part of Wall Street, as an executive with E. F. Hutton. He is a trustee of Wooster School. When he speaks, everyone *ought* to listen. He knows a lot. But I doubt that he is without prejudice. No more is Donald Schwartz. No more am I.

Unthinkable Thoughts
about Women

Why were most big things unladylike? Charlotte had once explained to her why. It was not that ladies were inferior to men; it was that they were different. Their mission was to inspire others to achievement rather than to achieve themselves. Indirectly, by means of tact and a spotless name, a lady could accomplish much. But if she rushed into the fray herself she would be first censured, then despised, and finally ignored. Poems had been written to illustrate this point.

There is much that is immortal in this medieval lady. The dragons have gone, and so have the knights, but still she lingers in our midst. She reigned in many an early Victorian castle, and was Queen of much early Victorian song. It is sweet to protect her in the intervals of business, sweet to pay her honour when she has cooked our dinner well. But alas! the creature grows degenerate. In her heart also there are springing up strange desires. She too is enamoured of heavy winds, and vast panoramas, and green expanses of the sea. She has marked the kingdom of this world, how full it is of wealth, and beauty, and war—a radiant crust, built around the central fires, spinning towards the receding heavens. Men, declaring that she inspires them to it, move joyfully over the surface, having the most delightful meetings with other men, happy, not because they are masculine, but because they are alive. Before the show breaks up she would like to drop the august title of the Eternal Woman, and go there as her transitory self.

Those thoughts were put into the mind of Lucy Honeychurch by her creator, E. M. Forster, in *A Room With a View*, written just ten years before I was born. I was brought up to be one of those men, inspired by such women as Lucy, to move joyfully over the surface of the earth. I found it sweet to protect my women, and to do them honor when they cooked my dinner well. My idea of the ideal woman was Helen of Troy, launching a thousand ships by her sheer beauty and feminine charm, not the late Ella Grasso, a great captain of her own ship. By my grandfather and my father and my father-in-law I was taught gallantry; that was the key—to smooth and pleasurable relationships with women. It has served me well. I don't know any man in the world who enjoys the company of women any more than I do. I love them and I want them to love me. So I do all the things that gallantry dictates, and do them happily. I stand up when they come into a room. I serve them cocktails, and dinner, and everything else, before I serve men. I hold their chair when they sit down at the table. I expect them to cook dinner, but I expect to carve. At social gatherings, some men seem naturally to gravitate to one side of the room with other men. I always "join the ladies," not just after dinner and following coffee and brandy and cigars, but immediately upon entering the room.

In spite of my desire to be in the presence of women, which I have had as long as I can remember (I fell in love for the first time when I was eight), I thought it no hardship to spend four years in an all-boys' boarding school and four more in an all-men's college. To me, business and pleasure were two different things, and it seemed perfectly natural to keep the two separate. Besides, it gave me an opportunity to write love letters, and sometimes to receive them. I think I almost believed at one point that boys and girls were invented so that they could exchange love letters. Henry Carlisle, in *The Contract*, puts into the mouth of a maiden aunt these delightful words: "I never allow myself to think about what goes on in a boys' school." What goes on in this respect is the idealization and adoration of females. Also, of course, their degradation—but that's merely the negative expression of the same thing.

One day I happened to arrive at a doorway at exactly the same instant as a young lady of my acquaintance, a young lady just about half my age. I stepped aside and held the door for her, as I had been taught to do for all ladies all my life, and as I even might well have done for another man. She stopped dead in her tracks, looked at me as though I had insulted her, and said, "What's this shit?" She was well known as an aggressive crusader for women's liberation, but even so I was startled out of my wits. Sometime later we had some conversations about the issue (though not the incident), and I came to understand that from her standpoint she *was* insulted. She took my gesture as an expression of that old-fashioned gallantry, designed centuries ago to keep women in their place (whether barefoot, pregnant, and in the kitchen or bedecked, bejeweled, and on a pedestal is in essence all the same). She might even have suspected me of a touch of mockery, since she knew that I knew what her feelings were. The fact is, of course, I never thought at all. The men who had taught me my brand of gallantry were the husbands and fathers of both my grandmothers, my mother, my two aunts, my sister, and my mother-in-law, none of whom had ever been to college. In all my life I had never given that fact much thought; but for my young friend in the doorway it was a burning issue.

French friends of mine, speaking of their youth, sometimes refer to it as *mon époque*. The pretentiousness of the phrase has always amused me. But in this context it is an apt phrase. The *époque* in which I was brought up started, as E. M. Forster pointed out, many years, indeed many centuries, before I was born. It may be coming to an end. That is why it seemed to me that the young lady in the doorway was insulting me, even as she felt that I was insulting her. Every one of my contemporaries—male and female alike—as well as others much younger than I, to whom I have told this story, have sided with me. They think that I was insulted, that I was right, and that the young lady was just plain rude. Of course she was, but that doesn't mean that she wasn't at least partly right. The rudeness could be explained in exactly the same terms as black militancy. Sometimes only shock treatment can bring about change. In the end she and I apologized to each other. I told her that I realized the insidiousness of gallantry (as I had been taught it), and she apologized to me, though I think it was not because I am a man but because I have white hair.

When the women's liberation movement first made the headlines, it hit me completely from the blind side. I was concentrating on race relations, and I had worked myself into such a lather on the subject that not only didn't I see women's liberation coming, I resented it when I finally realized that it had arrived. It seemed to me that it was a cheap bit of hitchhiking on the civil rights movement, which, as far as I was concerned, meant race relations, not sex relations. Compared with the blacks and the Chicanos, what did women have to complain about? None of the women I knew were involved in the movement, at least at the start, which meant that those who were must be crackpots. I was not alone. Every man I knew, as well as every woman I knew, took the same position. We were all of the same *époque*. Our unthinkable thoughts about women included women at West Point, women priests, and at Wooster a woman athletic director, a girl winner of our annual scholar-athlete award, and a girl senior prefect. Now all these things have come to pass, and I have come to believe that they are all as they should be, and that there are still many other unthinkable thoughts to be dealt with. Prejudice persists.

Wooster School's going coed is an even less earthshaking historical event than the acceptance of our first black students. But it provides a somewhat similar microcosm for understanding a phenomenon in our society. We accepted our first girl students fourteen years after our first black students, and it had nothing to do with women's liberation. What happened subsequently was very much intertwined with women's liberation, but not the initial decision. We were simply part of a vast national trend among the majority of independent schools, colleges, and universities that had previously been single-sex institutions. We all learned a lot in the process about the nature of prejudice, in this case not so much prejudice against as prejudice about. The trustee vote for Wooster to go coed was unanimous and was brought about by an almost unanimous petition from the students and faculty. Everyone was for it. Everyone was for females! We started with thirty-three, as compared with our having started with two blacks. We were so happy that we sang. Little did we (an all-male student body, an all-male board of trustees, and an all-but-one-male faculty) know how much we had to learn.

On the first day of school in the fall of 1970, we made our first mistake. We tried to organize the girls into a team of cheerleaders! We bought them sexy costumes and pompons and proceeded to teach them all the cheers and fetching routines. The boys sang. We all sang—except the girls. It seems that the boys—and the faculty—were still thinking along the lines of Lucy Honeychurch's cousin Charlotte: "Their mission was to inspire others to achievement rather than to achieve themselves." But the girls had come to achieve themselves. They didn't want to cheer the boys; they wanted to compete. Fortunately we gave up the idea quickly. To their credit, some of the girls refused, some tried it and quit, and the rest just grumped through the season, which is not what cheerleaders are supposed to do. We never went as far as the professional football teams in degrading females on the sidelines; but in principle we were guilty of the same thing. On commencement day the following spring, I apologized publicly to the girls for what we had tried to do and thanked them for having been uncooperative.

Earlier I have criticized athletics as a teaching device. But I have to say that our community learned more about our prejudice about women through ath-

letics than through any other area of our life together. Once the boys' varsity basketball coach got in
a heated debate in a faculty meeting about practice
time on the gym floor. He argued that his team was a
member of a league, that they had a fourteen-game
schedule, and that they simply had to have more practice time than the girls, who at that point had a kind
of informal pickup schedule with other schools in the
same situation. It was pointed out that maybe someday
the girls would also like to be in a league, with a similar
kind of schedule. Ten years later the girls *were* in a
league, a highly competitive league, and finished their
season with eleven wins and one loss. Since they were the
best team in the school that year, *everyone* cheered
them on—boys, girls, faculty, parents, and one retired
teacher (who never missed a game). That team was
coached by the former boys' coach, who had had such a
change of heart that, like all converts, he had become
something of a fanatic. That battle was won . . . but
there were others.

Wooster has always been what is called a self-help
school, which means that never in its history has it had
a single employee with what might be called janitorial
duties. The students clean the school every day, wait
on tables, wash the dishes, set up the dining room for
the next meal, and take care of the grounds. The entire
operation is supervised by various members of the
senior class. The faculty is not involved in any way
except when the system breaks down. The question
came up at the very outset as to just what a girl could
be expected to do. Illustrating that prejudice about
women was not limited to the older generation, the senior prefect and the headwaiter both came to me and
said that they were against having the girls wait on

tables. The boys wanted to wait on them! "But, sir! Girls can't carry those trays!" (That was years before the girls had won eleven out of twelve basketball games and before one of them had finally become senior prefect.) "Cheer us on to victory," they seemed to be saying, "and we'll wait on you." Gallantry . . . *mon époque.*

The senior prefect at Wooster is responsible for the entire self-help system, as well as being the number-one student in terms of maintaining discipline. He (she) is the official leader of the senior class and therefore is also indirectly responsible for the general morale of the place. He (she) is the official representative of the student body to the faculty and of the faculty to the student body. It is a big job, not to be confused in any way with what is generally thought of as "class president." Naturally, the question came up early as to whether or not a girl could be senior prefect. It took ten years before the answer was yes. When it finally was, she turned out to be black as well as a girl. Maybe that helped her; since the school had been racially integrated long before it was sexually integrated, it didn't hurt. But there were hurdles of prejudice (again more among the young than among the old) to be overcome before this historic event could come to pass.

Traditionally, the senior prefect is appointed by the headmaster, but only after many hours of discussion among the faculty and among the prefects of the graduating class. After about the third year of coeducation, one girl emerged as the possible senior prefect for the following year. I mentioned her name to the eleven students in my living room, ten of them boys and one girl. The boys argued vociferously. "Sir, a girl simply can't do that job." I thought they were kidding and threw out a few names like Golda Meir (who was doing fine at the time), and Catherine the Great, and Queen Victoria, and Madame Curie—all to no avail. Ella Grasso and Margaret Thatcher, unfortunately, were not yet ready to help us that day. The one girl in the room couldn't stand listening to the discussion for long and went out to the kitchen where my wife was trying to stay out of trouble and cried, "Mrs. Verdery, help! I can't believe it!" These boys were well-meaning, but deadly serious. It seemed that we still had a lot to teach —and learn.

The temptation is to write off this whole story as an illustration of the charming confusion of youth, "Aren't kids something, though? . . . Don't you love 'em? . . . Honestly, they kill me!" People who talk that way—and there are many of them—usually have nothing to do with the young and have forgotten that they were ever young themselves. People who deal constantly with the young know that they grow up and that in the process the charm seems to recede, leaving only the confusion. The integration of Wooster School as a coeducational institution involved a great many adults and a great many adult issues. Unquestionably there was just as much confusion here as among the young, and definitely less charm. The issue was women teachers and women administrators and women trustees.

Josette Eynon, whose husband became Wooster's fourth headmaster in 1980, had been on the faculty for years before the school went coed, so we went into the game with one experienced player, who also served as a coach. Though it is irrelevant, I cannot resist recording the headline in the school paper the year Josette joined the faculty: WOOSTER HIRES FIRST FULL-TIME FEMALE. Josette *is* a full-time female, not a flamboyant crusader for women's liberation, but a quiet and effective worker. First she worked on me. The issue was pay. (Whenever she and I arrive at a doorway at the same time, and I step aside and let her pass, she smiles, thanks me, and goes ahead.) My thinking on the subject of pay was typical of many headmasters in similar circumstances—blind, insensitive, and morally wrong. Because Wooster, like many a not-for-profit institution, was always short of funds, I reasoned that since her husband was well paid (by the standards of the time and the profession), and since he was provided with a house (in which his wife also lived), I had the makings of a bargain. No matter what I paid Josette, it was *pure gravy* for the family. Besides, there were some things she couldn't do—like coach a sport in an all-boys' school, check out dormitories at night, or serve as officer of the day (we used to use the phrase "master of the day," but since "mistress of the day" hardly seemed appropriate, for Josette's sake we changed). Josette argued otherwise. And she insisted that she could, would (and she did), put in as much time both in class and out of class as any man. Because part of her husband's recompense was in the form of housing, and because she was entitled to that same housing *as his wife*, and not as a member of the faculty, it could be that her cash salary might just have to be more than her husband's. What an unthinkable thought! Of course, pay became a major plank in the platform of women's liberation, but this was before those days. The point is that the relationship between Josette and me was friendly. I was a witness at her wedding and I baptized one of her children. The point is that I was well-meaning in my heart and *wanted* to do what was right. The point is that even so it took an enormous wrenching of the mind (and several years) for me to see the issue. The point is that prejudice persists.

In any case, when the day of coeducation arrived, we had already learned at least this lesson.

The question of female administrators and female trustees was more difficult. Here the issue was qualifications. There were plenty of qualified women teachers, if one could find them, pay them properly, and persuade them to join the team. But there were not plenty of qualified administrators and trustees. This was the fault of the world at large, of centuies of cousin Charlotte's fixation: "But if she rushed into the fray herself she would be first censured, then despised, and finally ignored. Poems had been written to illustrate this point." At one time Wooster School had on its board the chairman of Dillon Reed, the chairman of American Express, the chairman of North American Sugar, and the president of Corning Glass. It was partly because of those kinds of experiences that they were exceptional trustees. Until the world allows women the chance to hold such positions, the pool for highly qualified women trustees will remain smaller than the pool for men. And until girls' schools stop having male heads, and coed schools, and maybe even boys' schools, give a woman a chance, female administrators with qualifying past experience will also be a little harder to find than male ones. Prejudice persists.

One thing cousin Charlotte said is true: "It was not that ladies were inferior to men; it was that they were different." They may not be *as* different as cousin Charlotte thought, but they are different. Racial integration has as its cornerstone the proposition that, given equal opportunity, a black man can do anything a white man can do. That is not true of a man and a

woman. Women deserve equal rights and equal opportunities, but not quite for the same reason. They deserve them because they are equally human and equally
in need of opportunities and rights. But the differences go deeper than the color of skin. Many of the
girls who have been graduated from Wooster, like many
of their contemporaries, see themselves as liberated
women. They are out in the world now, fighting for
equal rights and opportunities. I am for that. But as
they get a little older, and as they marry and have
children, I notice a propensity among some to want it
both ways. I don't think this is a weakness on their
part, or a selling out. I think it is a subconscious grop-
ing with the fact of difference. We still have a lot to
teach—and a lot to learn, "before the show breaks up."

The Dreams of Youth

In the youth of every generation there is wonder about the nature and meaning of existence; there is wonder about one's self and one's relationship to something other—the cosmos, the universe, the sky, God; there is puzzlement about the things that seem to be wrong with the way the world is being run. There is, in other words, a natural mysticism born very early in the hearts of most people. And about the same time there is developed some sort of zeal to make over the world into something better. One characteristic of both this early mysticism and zeal is sentimentality. Another is optimism. A third is a distrust of compromise.

Every generation has its own causes, as well as its own vocabulary and style. I admit that although I was in sympathy with the causes of the generation of the sixties, I had trouble with their vocabulary and style. Even so I could see something of myself and my contemporaries in this now most famous (or infamous) of young generations. The only demonstration parade I ever marched in was in 1936, down Nassau Street, in Princeton, New Jersey. It was for the Veterans of Future Wars. We wanted our service bonuses before we were killed, instead of after. The salute was like the Hitler salute, except that the palm was up and open, the better to receive the money. Most of us were not serious, because most of us didn't really think there was going to be another war. The march on Selma and the burning of draft cards in the sixties was of a different order. But the underlying message was the same: "We don't like the way the older generation is running the world and we're going to do things better when we take over."

The story of my generation is that we meant to, and we tried, and we failed. And that will be the story of the generation of the sixties, and was the story of the generation of the twenties. Personally, I don't find that discouraging.

My own story bears telling, not because it is special, but precisely because it is not special. At the ages of twelve and thirteen I walked every morning from our apartment on Bank Street, in Greenwich Village, to school on 12th Street, just east of Seventh Avenue. On my way I passed a bread line, the sight of which deeply affected me. Down-and-outers selling apples on street corners were also a common sight. My stepfather had lost all his money in the Crash, and my father had lost his job. My stepmother supported my father on a minute teacher's salary, and my mother supported my stepfather by working at our school as a secretary. Life for all of us was something less than ideal; but it was still easy for me to see in the faces of the people standing in the bread line that others were worse off. Thus, at a relatively early age, I became aware that there was suffering in the world. A yearning to do something about it was born within me.

It was at about this time that I first fell under the spell of Donald Aldrich, who was to become my rector, then my sponsor for the ministry, then my employer, then my father-in-law, and always for me a special inspiration. It seemed to me that his life was devoted to alleviating suffering, and I liked that. When I went to Blair Academy to boarding school, I read Theodore Dreiser's *Sister Carrie* and made another discovery—that some of the suffering of some of the people in the world was caused by other people's cruelty and selfishness. So righteous indignation was born within me. The yearning and the indignation combined to form zeal.

Meanwhile, I was characteristically wondering about the meaning of life and my relationship to something other, which, because of the influence of Donald Aldrich, I chose to call God. So mysticism was born, and I was ready to go out and try to save the world.

Strangely enough, the rest of my high school years and my four years of college changed me very little in these respects, so that I arrived in seminary with my early zeal and mysticism pretty much in their original form. The sentimentality, of course, was there. God was kind and wise and very much concerned with me. And the optimism was there. I was confident the world could be saved and that I could play an important role.

In seminary my beliefs were quickly crystallized and changed. I learned a new phrase—the Social Gospel. And my God began to take on a sterner aspect. The great Julius Bewer, our Old Testament professor, who resembled the prophets about whom he lectured, introduced me to Amos and Isaiah and Jeremiah, among others. From Amos he read to us about God's plumb line. It is held against the wall, and if the wall is straight it will stand, and if it is not it will fall. That is justice. From Jeremiah he read to us of the plot of ground in Anathoth, which that prophet bought *after* the fall of Jerusalem to symbolize that there will be a future. That is faith. From Isaiah he read to us of the angels who touched that prophet's lips with burning coals to purify them, after which Isaiah cried, "Here am I. Send me." That is zeal. And all of this was against the background of a world now being torn apart by war. My response to this God became less sentimental.

Because of the nature of a theological seminary, coupled with the atmosphere of war, it was natural that all elements of the dreams of youth should heighten—the yearning, the indignation, the zeal, and the mysticism. Reinhold Niebuhr and Paul Tillich were handing out strong medicine, beside which the preaching of Donald Aldrich, in whose church I was then a student assistant, seemed naïve and silly. As a hero he was beginning to tarnish. I had had some suspicions of this as early as in my *Sister Carrie* days. It troubled me, as I wrote my mother at the time, that our rector was saving the world in a chauffeur-driven limousine. My mother explained to me, in a letter that I still have, that he could get around the city faster and see and help more people with a car and chauffeur than in any other way, thus introducing me to the notion of efficacy—and compromise. I was not convinced, but because I loved my mother and needed my hero, I kept an open mind. Now, with friends of mine going off to prison rather than cooperate with the war effort by registering for the draft, I had deeply serious doubts. *Efficacy* and *compromise* seemed like very bad words to me, and to my friends. Then suddenly, one day, Donald Aldrich fooled us. He left his comfortable New York parish and at the age of fifty-two enlisted in the navy (for the second time in his life). He spent the rest of the war in the South Pacific, as a chaplain.

And I went off to a small school in New England to work out my own salvation, or, as my sons would say a generation later, "do my thing."

In the sentimentality of my early youth, I kept a notebook of quotations that appealed to me. The only one I remember is from Marcus Aurelius: "Keep true to the dreams of thy youth." The reason I remember it is that the dreams of youth have always seemed so very important to me, even though I have learned long since that not many people, if any, ever succeed in keeping true to them. That is partly because the dreams of youth are dreams, not yet touched by the other realities of life; which is not to say that they are irrelevant. It is a form of defeat, I think, to abandon them altogether; but they must be reconciled. The story of my life—perhaps anybody's life—is the story of that reconciliation. In the forty years since I first began to feel my youthful dreams slipping a little out of my control, I have learned three things: that a little is better than nothing; that nothing is ever enough; and that compromise can be beautiful.

I wrote a letter to my firstborn grandchild, Amanda, on the very day of her birth to welcome her into our world. I said, in part, "You have already breathed some of our air, and taken some of our nourishment, and are taking up some of our space. So you are already in debt. I hope that you will discover that finding ways to repay that debt, according to your own style, can be one of the great joys of your life." As this book goes to press, Amanda is just beginning to learn to speak, so we do not know what kind of dreams she is having, or what her relationship seems to her to be to something other than herself, or how dissatisfied she may already be with the way we (her parents and her grandparents and our contemporaries) are running the world. But it is safe to assume that sometime, before very long, she will have dreams, and that in essence they will not be so very different from the ones we have had, and that she will indeed find fault with the way we have done things. And we must hope that she will want to correct some of our mistakes. We must also hope that she will never know despair, that she will never stop trying, that she will never allow herself to believe that her efforts are useless. If the world is ever going to be saved, Amanda must grow up to believe, and continue to believe all her life, that doing something is better than doing nothing.

A few years ago, Wooster School launched a major financial campaign, for $3½ million. We appealed to everyone we knew, which included a fourteen-year-old girl who was then studying in France for the year. She was on a scholarship, with a pittance for spending money. What must a campaign for $3½ million have looked like to her? Obviously, it looked exactly like being asked to save the world. She sent me $3, along with a beautiful letter: ". . . *Cette année, j'ai decidé que je suis assez agée maintenant pour donner l'argent à quelque chose qui m'est très cher. Et Wooster m'est très, très, cher. Je sais que $3.00 ne sont pas beaucoup, mais je pense qu'un peu est mieux que rien. . . . Je vous embrasse.*"

"*Un peu est mieux que rien.*" In any language I believe that is a profoundly important truth, not at all self-evident. It is so easy, and so tempting, to believe the contrary, that if a little is not enough, then it is *not* better than nothing; that it *is*, in effect, nothing, maybe even worse than nothing, because it gives the illusion of progress. But a little is a gesture, a way of speaking, a way of life.

Shortly before he was to be crucified, Jesus was staying with a friend into whose house a woman suddenly entered with an alabaster jar of precious ointment. To the consternation of those standing around, she broke the jar and poured the contents over Jesus' head. Why? What a useless thing to do! The ointment might better have been sold and the money given to the poor. But Jesus saw it differently. In one of my favorite lines in the New Testament he said, simply, "She has done what she could." To save the world, that is the only place to start.

There is another story of Jesus with quite a different ending. It is the story of rich young man who very much wanted to do what is right. He wanted to know "what good deed" he should do in order to inherit eternal life. He was told that he must keep the Ten Commandments, plus love God with all his heart and soul and his neighbor as himself. The young man replied that he was already faithful in all these regards, which was more of a mouthful than anyone I know could honestly reply. Pressed for more of an answer, Jesus said, "If you would be perfect, go, sell what you possess and give to the poor, and you will have treasure in heaven: and come, follow me." The story ends on a sad note, sad for the young man and sad for many of the rest of the world: "When the young man heard this, he went away sorrowful; for he had great possessions."

It is important to know that a little is better than nothing, that to do what one can is at least something. But it is equally important to know that nothing is ever enough.

One story about Donald Aldrich has never ceased

to intrigue me, delight me, and puzzle me. A young man who had once been a member of the children's choir at the Church of the Ascension enlisted in the paratroops at the age of eighteen. Shortly thereafter the war ended, so that he found himself, like many thousands of others, faced with the boring task of being trained to fight a war that was over. He was stationed in Louisiana, and one night he went carousing with his friends in the nearest small town, got drunk, and drove his army jeep through the plate-glass window of a local store. There had been a series of such incidents between that town and the nearby army base, and the civilian judge who heard the case had run out of patience. He sentenced the young man to twenty years in prison.

Donald Aldrich, who by then was a bishop, decided that the sentence was inexcusably excessive and that he was going to do something about it. The season was midsummer, and he knew that it would be very hot in Louisiana. He bought himself a palm beach suit, a panama hat, a clerical collar (which up to then he had neither owned nor worn), and a Pullman ticket to New Orleans. He then called a prominent banker he knew in that city and said, "I'm coming down your way and I would like to meet Governor Huey Long." His banker friend had no trouble arranging such a meeting, and Donald Aldrich, perhaps the handsomest and suavest man of his time, snowed the governor. Eventually, of course, in their utterly friendly conversation over lunch at Antoine's, the subject of the young man in prison came up, and, of course, the young man was pardoned.

Now is that the way to save the world?

Not according to the dreams of anybody's youth. There is a cynicism about the story that is very nearly shocking. The bishop was too much of the world to save the world. All he did was play the governor's game, with the deck rather stylishly stacked. There was no crusade. Injustice, the real enemy, was never openly faced.

At the same time, the story has a certain soap-opera charm. Between the bishop and the governor there was a good guy–bad guy plot that had all the moral simplicity of a soap opera. And there is the inner satisfaction (which makes some people soap-opera fans) of knowing from the outset that the good guy is going to win. As soon as the bishop sets his panama hat on his head at a rakish angle, we all begin to cheer for virtue. *In addition*, there *was* a relatively innocent eighteen-year-old boy, doomed to twenty years in prison, who was set free after only six months. In his own way, the bishop had done what he could. What's wrong with that?

In sharp contrast to the story of the bishop and the governor, with its amusing charm, is the deeply moving story of the French mountain village of Le Chambon, so brilliantly told by Phillip Hallie in *Lest Innocent Blood Be Shed* (Harper & Row, 1979). Magda Trocmé, wife of the local Protestant pastor, André Trocmé, is cooking dinner on a cold winter's evening in 1940, during the Nazi occupation of France. The front door, which is never locked, opens and reveals the forlorn, half-starved, half-frozen figure of a Jewish woman, who wants to know if she can come in. Without an instant's hesitation, Madame Trocmé says, "Naturally, come in and come in." The incident launches a four-year story of the courage and self-sacrifice of an entire village, which, under the leadership of the Trocmés and others, is transformed under the very noses of the Nazis into the safest place for Jewish and other refugees in all of Europe. There are heroes and heroines by the score, as well as some martyrs; and there are lives saved by the thousands.

Now is that the way to save the world?

Certainly it is morally more impressive than the story of the bishop and the governor, and more consistent with the dreams of youth. But there are two difficulties. The first is that too few of us have the courage and the will for self-sacrifice to follow that model. We are inspired by the Trocmés of this world, but we end up like the rich young man, going away sorrowful. And the second difficulty is that even what the people of Le Chambon did is not enough.

George Bernard Shaw is credited with having said, "The trouble with Christianity is not that it has been tried and found wanting, but that it has never been tried." That is clever, but I do not believe that it is true. I think that St. Francis of Assisi not only tried Christianity but came closer to making it work than perhaps anyone else who ever lived. I also think that the Trocmés and the other people of Le Chambon tried to make Christianity work. I even think the bishop tried. I think my friend Peter Fine, who didn't even call himself a Christian, tried, along with quite a few others mentioned in these pages.

But nothing is ever enough. Even the people of Le Chambon were troubled in their conscience by the fact that for four years they forged false identification papers, and by the fact that they did not succeed in saving the lives of everyone who came to their doors to be saved.

How can one reconcile the paradox that a little is better than nothing, but that nothing is ever enough? The word is *compromise*.

Among the young of the generation of the sixties,

the word *compromise* was a dirty one. To them it meant to give in, to stop trying, to sell out. It was to them the whole trouble with the world! But so was it to me at the same age, and to my friends. So was it to my father, in his youth. And so has it been to my sons and to all the students I have known over the past forty years. So will it be, I am sure, to my granddaughter, Amanda, even before she learns how to spell it. The dreams of youth are dreams. Somehow, sometime, they have to be confronted with those other realities of life, and compromise is the only alternative to despair.

But there is more, and a better thing to say. I have come to believe that compromise can be beautiful. It means to accommodate (not such a bad concept), to give a little (as opposed to giving in). Literally, it means to *promise with.* As one moves into adulthood, one takes his dreams and accommodates them—to other people and their dreams (and their needs), as well as to the relative merits of causes. One does the best one can and then acknowledges that that is not enough. Those who are stronger, like St. Francis and the Trocmés, give some of their strength to those who are weaker, partly by inspiration and partly by keeping them honest—that is to say, never satisfied with themselves.

Callousness, indifference, self-pity, and despair are the great enemies of society. They are not naturally part of the dreams of youth. They are acquired as we carry our young dreams into the world the way it is. They are designed to protect our dreams, to keep us from waking up, as though the purity of the dreams were sacred. But a pure dream is nothing but a pure dream. To be alive means to be awake, to try to remember the dream, if it was a good one (which in itself is not always easy), and then to translate it into the realities of being alive—in an imperfect world that needs improving.

The great compromise of life is the promise that we make with God (if we are comfortable with him), or with society, or with life. We promise to do what we can and never to be satisfied. But the promise is *with* that other party, whatever we may call it or however we may conceive of it. In return for our promise, we receive the promise of God, which happens to be the word that I use. It comes in the form of pleasure with our efforts and forgiveness for our falling short. In religious terms that is called redemption. In non-religious terms it is a deep-seated feeling, not of self-satisfaction, but of contentment.

Acknowledgments

ACKNOWLEDGMENTS have always seemed to me to be a bit liturgical in nature—essential to the production, but more formula than feeling. When I was a student assistant at St. Paul's Cathedral in Boston, we used to put on a pretty good show of a Sunday morning. We had a great organist, a fine boys' choir and men's choir, people moving around the chancel who more or less knew what they were doing, often some very distinguished guests, and, in our dean, Edwin Van Etten, one of the great preachers of those times. When we finally all arrived in the sacristy after the last verse of the recessional hymn, self-satisfaction tended to run rampant. Then the dean, in a booming voice, would pray for us all. "Not unto us, O Lord, not unto us, but unto Thy name be the praise." It was, like acknowledgments in books, the only decent thing to say after what we all knew had been a good performance.

181

Anyone who has nerve enough to write a book must think he has something to say worth saying and that he is capable of putting words together more or less clearly and persuasively. Then, if the effort ends up in print, it follows that someone else agrees with him. That's heady, and so acknowledgments were invented to introduce a note of modesty—false or otherwise, depending on the tone and style of the liturgy.

All acknowledgments say basically the same thing: "I couldn't have done it alone." That's a nice thing to say, because it is true; but sometimes the elaboration gets out of hand. There is the school that chants, "Everything good about this book is due to So-and-So and So-and-So. But for everything that's bad or wrong, I take all the blame." To this the reader is supposed to say, "Oh, come on, you've got to be kidding! You're too modest!"—which, of course, no author is.

Handing out kudos is a nice way to pass the time, especially if they are handed to people one likes. The problem is to know where to begin and where to end. An easy way out would be to say, "Not unto us, O Lord, not unto us, but unto Thy name be the praise." But I would like the pleasure of naming some names.

Because I am not a professional writer, I'd like to start with those people in the profession who encouraged and helped me. First and foremost is the Reiss family. The late Malcolm was my agent even before it had occurred to me that there would be any place in my life for a literary agent. After his death, his son Bill succeeded him in the delicate assignment of constantly trying to persuade me that I could write. Because Bill had once been a student of mine, the task was the more delicate for him. This is to acknowledge that he has carried it out with a grace worthy of his father. Then Atheneum, in its infinite wisdom, assigned Lucia Reiss, Bill's mother, as my editor.

Lucia Reiss, like her husband and her son, is a professional in the literary world. Her job was to take on an amateur and try to make him read like a professional. Others merely had to encourage. She had to doctor, both the text and the author. The medicines she prescribed were always given in small doses, so as not to upset the system—patience as a steady diet, repetition after every meal, a gentle reminder before bed, and never a bitter pill. The harshest thing I ever had to swallow was a phrase written once in the margin opposite a paragraph: "Not very good writing." Everything else was sugar-coated with "I wonder if you could . . ." "Don't you think you might try . . ." "Are you sure this is what you mean? . . ." "Let's try this part again."

Sometimes she had to operate. For anesthetic she used charm, so there never was any pain. Lucia Reiss has made it fun for me to go back to school again, after all these years of merely running a school.

First among the nonprofessionals is my wife, who guarded my study door and the phone for hundreds of hours, who read everything in two or three different forms, always with helpful additions and even more helpful subtractions, who listened ad nauseam while I answered the question over and over again, "Tell me, what is your book *about?*" Having lived with me through everything in the book during our nearly forty years of married life, she knew more than she needed to know, but still managed sometimes to act as though some things, some ideas, were new to her.

Next is Anne Pérouse, of the American embassy in Paris, who volunteered to type the entire first draft from an original manuscript that was not easy reading.

If Paris were not so unhandy to Ridgefield, Connecticut, she would have insisted on typing the final draft as well. As a matter of fact, during a week's vacation with us she did type some of it. But because Paris is so unhandy, and Anne is usually there, I am grateful to Christine Voltmer (of handy Ridgefield) for completing that thankless chore.

Lest anyone who has read this far should think that I am surrounded only by women, let me acknowledge that among the people who read all or part of the manuscript, two of the most helpful were my colleague Donald Schwartz and my former student Edward Gunn.

This brings me to the final acknowledgment, not to those who helped me write the book, but to those who, to paraphrase Yogi Berra, helped "make this book necessary"—the army of friends, colleagues, students, parents, and members of my own family who have made me want to recall, if only partially, what my life has been about. But the list is too long, so finally I'll just say, "Not unto us, O Lord, not unto us. . . ."

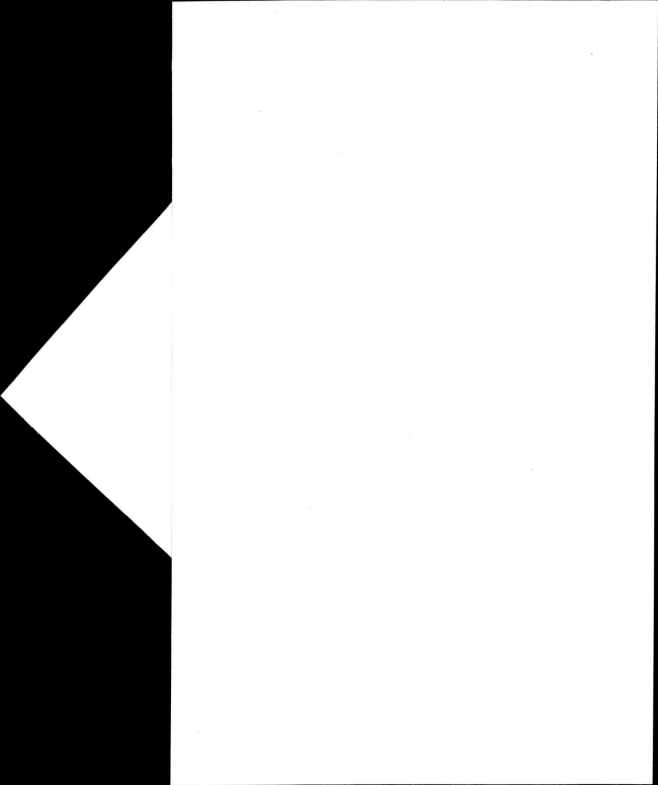

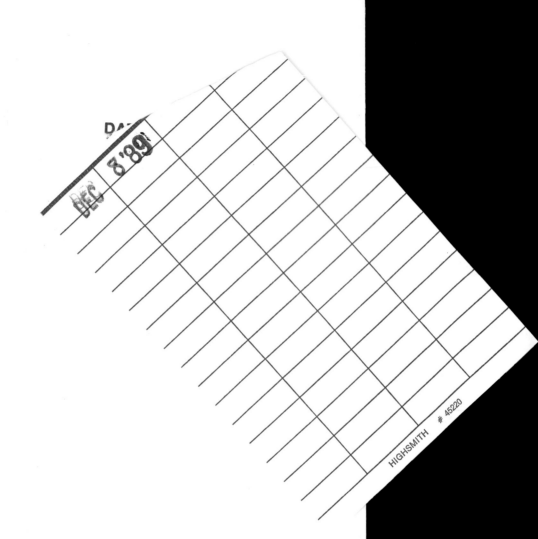